THE EDUCATIONAL PRACTICES AND PATHWAYS OF SOUTH AFRICAN STUDENTS

across power-marginalised spaces

EDITED BY ASLAM FATAAR

SUN PRESS

*The Educational Practices and Pathways of South African Students
across Power-Marginalised Spaces*

Published by AFRICAN SUN MeDIA under the SUN PReSS imprint

This publication was subjected to an independent double-blind peer evaluation by the publisher.

The authors and the publisher have made every effort to obtain permission for and acknowledge the use of copyrighted material. Refer all enquiries to the publisher.

Views reflected in this publication are not necessarily those of the publisher.

First edition 2018

ISBN 978-1-928357-88-9
ISBN 978-1-928357-89-6 (e-book)
https://doi.org/10.18820/9781928357896

Set in PT Serif 10/14
Cover design, typesetting and production by AFRICAN SUN MeDIA

SUN PReSS is a licensed imprint of AFRICAN SUN MeDIA. Scholarly, professional and reference works are published under this imprint in print and electronic formats.

This publication can be ordered from:
orders@africansunmedia.co.za
Takealot: bit.ly/2monsfl
Google Books: bit.ly/2k1Uilm
africansunmedia.store.it.si (e-books)
Amazon Kindle: amzn.to/2ktL.pkL

Visit africansunmedia.co.za for more information.

Contents

Chapter 7

Back from the edge: Exploring adult education and training
as second chance opportunity for adult students

Chapter 8

"The writing's on the wall ... and in other forbidden places":
Youth using languaging practices to mediate the past in
formal and informal learning spaces

Chapter 9

Prompting students' learning dispositional adaptation
in response to teachers' pedagogical practices in a
township school

List of
Contributors

ADAM COOPER is a Research Specialist at the Human Sciences Research Council, Cape Town office.

DORIA DANIELS is a Professor in the Department of Educational Psychology at Stellenbosch University.

NAZLI DOMINGO-SALIE is a Deputy Chief Education Specialist in the Institutional Management and Governance Planning Directorate in the Western Cape Education Department, Cape Town.

ASLAM FATAAR is a distinguished Professor in the Department of Education Policy Studies at Stellenbosch University. He is the outgoing President of the South African Education Research Association.

JENNIFER FELDMAN is a Research Associate in the Department of Education Policy Studies, Stellenbosch University.

HENRY FILLIES is Deputy Principal at Charleston Hill Secondary School, Paarl, Cape Town.

NAJWA NORODIEN-FATAAR is a Lecturer and acting Head of Department in the Fundani Centre of Higher Education and Development at the Cape Peninsula University of Technology, Cape Town.

ELZAHN RINQUEST is Head of Department at Jan Kriel School, Kuils River, Cape Town.

BATANDWA SONAMZI is Principal of Welwitschia Primary School in Delft South, Cape Town.

Acknowledgements

This book is the result of ongoing work with a group of our graduated students (Batandwa, Henry, Nazli, Elzahn, Adam and Jennifer) in the Department of Education Policy Studies at Stellenbosch University and two invited chapter contributors, namely Professor Doria Daniels and doctoral graduand Najwa Norodien-Fataar, in the Department of Educational Psychology at Stellenbosch University.

I would like to acknowledge the quality and depth of intellectual effort of each chapter contributor and thank them in bringing this book to fruition.

We wrote this book in an engaging and exciting conversation that stretched over a two-year period.

I extend my gratitude to Marie Brennan and Lew Zipin for their generous Foreword, and our ongoing mixed mode conversations regarding ways of developing conceptual languages that advance social and educational justice in complex times.

I gratefully acknowledge the support and generosity of South Africa's National Research Foundation (NRF), which funded the research for this book, grant no. CPRR13082831319.

I would like to thank AFRICAN SUN MeDIA for their assistance in preparing the manuscript for publication.

I dedicate this book to the children on whose stories the research presented here is based.

ASLAM FATAAR

Foreword

Studying South African savage inequalities in search of robust social-educational justice

Lew Zipin & Marie Brennan

South Africa's starkly segregated spatial geographies – impoverished and prosperous settlements only short distances apart – correlate with gross disparities in education provisions, thus displaying what Kozol (1991) famously referred to as 'savage inequalities'. In his research across city districts of the 'advanced capitalist' United States of the 1980s, Kozol studied how intersecting class-race structures of unequal power reflect in sharply distinct demographics, linked to school resource disparities, across neighbourhoods in close proximity. From statistical and ethnographic data, Kozol provided relational analysis of how schools in well-off and 'white' areas held gross educational advantages over schools in zones populated by poor and mainly African-American or Latino groups. Kozol's primary focus was on resource inequalities across schools, highlighting what Fraser (2009) calls the *redistributive* element of social justice: that justice requires redistributing crucial resources – which power-marginalised groups lack *systemically* (i.e. through no 'deficit' of their own) – to support educational access, engagement and success.

Some thirty years later, in the 'post-colonial' South African context of areas around Cape Town and Stellenbosch, *The Educational Practices and Pathways of South African Students across Power-Marginalised Spaces* (*TEPP*) likewise highlights savage inequalities. In addition to *redistribution*, educational focus is given to the remaining two of Fraser's '3R' principles for pursuing robust social justice: *recognition*, by inclusion in the curriculum, of students' cultural-historic heritages and codes; and participatory *representation*, from all groups whose lives are subjected to educational institutions, in decisions that determine what knowledge-abilities are taught-and-learned. Emergent questions include: How do educational settings *mis*-recognise the learning capacities of students from power-marginalised spaces as embodying 'deficits in 'natural ability' or 'cultural functionality'? How might education instead *recognise* value, and make curricular and pedagogic use of the social-cultural assets in these students' lifeworlds? Can educational practices thus change, rather than reproduce, what Appadurai (2004) calls 'the terms of recognition'? (We note that both Appadurai's and Fraser's conceptual framings are taken up in various chapters of *TEPP*, as tools for analyses of ethnographic findings.)

TEPP authors approach these questions through ethnographic studies, paying qualitative attention to connections across lifeworld and educational settings, thereby illuminating how social and educational spaces interact in subjective and cultural processes by which power-marginalised young people form learning dispositions, along with senses of how educational institutions may or may not serve their and their communities' needs and aspirations. In so doing, authors elucidate social-educational features of a 'post-colonised' and 'post-apartheid' South Africa that need to be distinguished from (so-called) 'first-world' nations.

It is important to take into consideration that inequalities are far more savage in South Africa. In this 'wealthiest African nation', at best 20% – mainly Anglo and Afrikaner (but not all) – still live in conditions of economic prosperity. Despite having a 'majority' government since 1994, most of SA's roughly 75% 'Black' and 9% 'Coloured' communities (by 2011 census categories) live in extreme poverty. Such structural steepness in South Africa's 'race'/class-entwined dynamics of inequality far exceeds that of Australia or the USA (with less 'trickle-down' in South Africa than what reaches 'internally colonised' groups in first-world nations). Close attention thus needs to be paid to specificities of South African inequalities – and how educational institutions and policy 'reform' efforts are implicated – within cross-national conversations on how best to understand and redress social-educational injustices on a local and, relationally, global level.

This is a critical time for South Africa, as a 'post-colonised' nation where justice is long overdue to, and demanded by, the diverse majority of power-marginalised groups, while 'majority' government appears inadequate to the task of addressing their needs and aspirations. 2016's university student protests, demanding that *fees must fall* and *curriculum must be decolonised*, are not mere moments of catharsis, we suggest, but signify deep disturbances with the educational status quo that has not made good on promises, for most, of pathways out of impoverished and racialised segregations that persist well into the 'post-apartheid' era. More ructions are likely, not just in universities but in other education sectors, so long as South Africa's savage inequalities fester unabated. It is an important juncture, then, for rethinking how education research can contribute to ongoing struggles for robust justice, with close qualitative attention to furthering the prospects of power-marginalised groups, not just in 'mainstream' educational sites but also spaces of experiment with vocational and alternative education. Indeed, several *TEPP* authors do undertake combinations of ethnographic and proactive research in such sites, on which they report in their respective chapters.

If South Africa's educational institutions and contexts express regionally distinctive aspects of savage inequality, they also express trends of globalising convergence. This travel from geographic 'centres' of advanced capitalism to 'peripheries' that are now supposedly 'post'-colonised, continue to be colonised, through supra-national exertions such as performance 'standards' and measurement criteria from the OECD. Withal the post-1994 mandates designing education around social-justice mandates, trends from the USA, UK and Australia have been borrowed into every major SA curriculum reform of the past few decades, including the current Curriculum Assessment Policy Statements (CAPS) (Fataar 2006; Zipin, Fataar & Brennan 2015). Various *TEPP* authors observe that CAPS, in fact, selects primarily for those already privileged by academic success. Such travelling of policy elements from wider geographies confounds efforts to redress distinctively SA-based features of savage inequality that pose challenges for the pursuit of social-educational justice by SA's power-marginalised learners, their communities, as well as their educators.

Nevertheless, education features borrowed from global power 'centres' make relevant the use of conceptual-analytical tools from geographies outside of South Africa – provided they are adapted to South African contexts. Across *TEPP* chapters, authors take up, test and re-think conceptual tools that travel into the country's education research, in search of explanatory power to elucidate SA-based conditions of possibility. Most prominent are Bourdieu's concepts of '*habitus*' and '*capital*', invoked in all but one chapter (authors cite many of Bourdieu's texts, too numerous to reference here: e.g. 1984, 1986, 1990, etc.).

Habitus is Bourdieu's concept for an embodied locus of subjective dispositions, cultured early in life, that guide perception of and response to further life, e.g. schools. Depending on whether habitus is cultured in relatively power-elite or power-marginalised family and neighbourhood contexts, it is apt to respond familiarly or in alienated ways to codes of expectation instituted in education settings. Yet, *TEPP* authors consistently invoke a concept of 'learning habitus' that is more heterogeneous and flexible in its dispositions. In this, they draw on work by SA educationist Fataar (e.g. 2010, 2015), who offers rich illustrations and analysis of how subjectivities among many youth are shaped by vicissitudes of a power-marginalised life that move them across diverse and shifting post-apartheid terrains of urban and rural space. Such mobility across patchwork habitats does not fit the more or less consistent family-neighbourhood settings that Bourdieu conceives. Appadurai (1996:55–56) poses a post-colonial challenge (on which Fataar draws):

> [S]ome of the force of Bourdieu's idea of the habitus can be retained ... [but] stress must be put on his idea of improvisation ... [which] no longer occurs

within a relatively bounded ... [terrain] but is always skidding and taking off ... [T]he glacial undertow of habitus ... [is thus rethought] in the face of lifeworlds that are frequently in flux.

Capital is another Bourdieuan concept both taken up and tested in *TEPP*. Bourdieu retains the Marxian sense of *capital* as possession of substances or qualities carrying strong exchange-value for market investment. For a substance/quality thus to function as *capital*, it must be: (a) scarce, and difficult to access, for most (power-marginalised) social groups; and (b) already accumulated in large amounts by more restricted (power-elite) groups. Bourdieu conceives educational institutions as 'markets' for '*cultural* capital'. The most effective of such *capital* being the dispositions, or habitus, that students from power-elite groups embody early in life, and that have become coded into key devices of institutional education – curricula, pedagogies, assessments, and more – as 'standards' from which those devices select. As a result, the dispositions embodied by young people from power-elite social-structural positions are selected as 'winning' *capital* in contests of mainstream school performance; whereas dispositions embodied in power-marginalised positions are rejected as 'lacking what it takes'. In sum, only limited cultural dispositions – those of power-elite groups – carry *exchange*-value (i.e. as *capital*), relative to dispositions that, in Marxist terms, may carry rich *use*-value in the lives of power-marginalised groups but not *exchange*-value in schools (Delpit 1995, Zipin 2015).

Such arbitrary privileging of 'elite' over 'marginalised' cultural codes is unacceptably unjust and *TEPP* authors find Bourdieu's concepts of *habitus* and *capital* helpful to explain how mainstream SA education – both like and unlike 'northern' geographies – select for success of the few, as against the many. Yet, Bourdieu's tools do not offer equivalent help to imagine how to transform and drive SA (or 'northern') education in a direction that is socially just – which is a driving ethical impulse within *TEPP* authors' research and analysis. In search of conceptual ballast, many *TEPP* authors take up Yosso's essay: "Whose culture has capital? A critical race theory discussion of community cultural wealth" (2005). While Yosso's scholarship also emerges from 'the global north' (the USA), she writes from 'subaltern' standpoints of groups subjected to internal colonisation, most saliently along a 'race' axis of power inequality, the dynamics of which, according to Critical Race Theory, must be analysed in intersection with class, gender and other axes of relational power asymmetry. From these standpoints, Yosso argues that strong *assets* for collective agency or community *wealths* have emerged as cultural-historical capacities among power-marginalised groups: capacities to recognise and resist devices of injustice; to aspire imaginatively towards futures of greater justice; and more. However, in also defining these *wealths* as *capitals* of alternative species to Bourdieu's, Yosso, in our view, makes a category error that loses the explanatory power of Bourdieu's (and Marx's) concept of *capital* as *'properties' by which privileges of the already-powerful are unjustly reproduced*. We raise this issue for, in our reading, various *TEPP* authors struggle with confoundings between Bourdieu's and Yosso's meanings of *capital*, often blending respective usages of the term without teasing apart their conceptual tensions.

Yet, *TEPP* authors wrestle productively with tensions across Yosso's and Bourdieu's concepts, in application to SA social-educational contexts. Very much to the point, we suggest that the robust conceptual contribution of Yosso's *wealths* is in the insight that power-marginalised groups embody collective capacities of far more value, in pursuing justice than *capitals*: *capacities for agency to challenge and change the game of capital selection*. Stemming from collective cultural-historical experiences in power-marginalised social spaces, they have accumulated: (a) an understanding of how savage inequalities operate in their communities and education settings; and (b) ethical-political imagination to pursue more robustly just social-educational arrangements. If Bourdieu's *capital* offers explanatory power for *TEPP* authors to analyse how mainstream South African education reproduces savage inequalities, then Yosso's *wealths* (if we don't also call them *capitals*) assist them to establish how, in educational research and practice, *to work with communities of the power-marginalised, towards education for robust justice*.

In highlighting wealths of capacity in SA's power-marginalised communities, *TEPP* does not lose sight of savage legacies of colonialism, slavery and capitalism. The authors do not pretend to 'solve' savage inequalities at the root of educational injustice. What they do offer – to both insiders, and to outsiders such as ourselves – is insight into the needs and aspirations that lie at the heart of struggles for justice in South Africa's educational system, and some options for research, policy and practice that warrant further investigation.

Lew Zipin is an Extraordinary Professor, Faculty of Education, Stellenbosch University, South Africa and Adjunct Senior Research Fellow, School of Education, University of South Australia, Adelaide, Australia.

Marie Brennan is an Extraordinary Professor, Faculty of Education, Stellenbosch University, South Africa and Adjunct Professor, School of Education, University of South Australia, Adelaide, Australia.

References

Appadurai A. 1996. *Modernity at large: Cultural dimensions of globalization.* Minneapolis: The University of Minnesota Press.

Appadurai A. 2004. "The capacity to aspire: culture and the terms of recognition". In: V. Rao & M. Walton (eds). *Culture and public action.* California: Stanford University Press.

Bourdieu P. 1984. *Distinction: A social critique of the judgement of taste.* Cambridge: Harvard University Press.

Bourdieu P. 1986. "The forms of capital". In: J. Richardson (ed). *Handbook of theory and research for sociology and education.* New York: Greenwood. 241–258.

Bourdieu P. 1990. *The logic of practice,* R. Nice (trans). Cambridge: Polity.

Delpit L. 1995. *Other people's children: Cultural conflict in the classroom.* New York: The New Press.

Fataar A. 2006. Policy networks in recalibrated political terrain: The case of school curriculum policy and politics in South Africa. *Journal of Education Policy,* 21(6): 641–659. https://doi.org/10.1080/02680930600969159

Fataar A. 2010. Youthful becoming and rural-urban mobility: the case of Fuzile Ali at a Muslim community school in Cape Town. *Southern African Review of Education,* 15(2):105–117.

Fataar A. 2015. *Engaging schooling subjectivities across post-apartheid urban spaces.* Stellenbosch: AFRICAN SUN MeDIA. https://doi.org/10.18820/9781920689834

Fraser N. 2009. *Scales of justice: Reimagining political space in a globalizing world.* New York: Columbia University Press.

Kozol J. 1991. *Savage inequalities: Children in America's schools.* New York: Crown Publishers.

SA Stats 2017. *Poverty trends in South Africa: An examination of absolute poverty between 2006 and 2015.* Pretoria: Statistics South Africa.

Yosso T. 2005. Whose culture has capital? A critical race theory discussion of community cultural wealth. *Race, Ethnicity and Education,* 8(1):69–91. https://doi.org/10.1080/1361332052000341006

Zipin L. 2015. Chasing curricular justice: How complex ethical vexations of redistributing cultural capital bring dialectics to the door of aporia. *Southern African Review of Education,* 21(2):91–109.

Zipin L, Fataar A & Brennan M. 2015. Can social realism do social justice? Debating the warrants for curriculum knowledge selection. *Education as Change,* 19(2):9–36. https://doi.org/10.1080/16823206.2015.1085610

Chapter 1

Introducing the terms of (mis)recognition in respect of students' educational practices across power-marginalised spaces

Aslam Fataar

Very little is known regarding the way students, who enter our schools, universities and colleges, exercise their educational agency across their multifarious lifeworlds. An understanding of who they are and how they 'practise their education' remains elusive, in effect, constituting a somewhat 'visible invisibility'. A view of students as multi-dimensional educational beings is buried underneath generalised statistical portrayals of achievement, dominant educational discourses, and extant institutional operations. This book offers an exploration of the educational practices and pathways of selected South African students and drives an argument about the complexity, nature and extent of their investment in educational futures amidst troubled social circumstances. It posits that only a qualitative engagement with the depth and richness of students' practices would allow for fuller educational recognition and institutional inclusion.

The book turns on an understanding of students' practices and educational pathways as actively constructed in and across 'power-marginalised spaces'. Such an understanding considers the social-relational elements at play in the accumulation of practices in impoverished contexts. In this regard, the notion 'power-marginalised' (Zipin, Fataar & Brennan 2015) emphasises the need to "get beyond normatively-loaded words such as 'disadvantage' or 'low socio-economic status' (SES), as well as words such as 'high-poverty' which tend to signify 'class' primarily, and not other social-relational axes of power asymmetry such as 'race', 'gender', and so on" (Zipin, personal communication, October 2017). It signifies the range of social-structural power relations that are articulated in respect of human practices in specific contexts. I argue that these relations play out in the light of complex social-spatial processes which extend across the different spaces of students' lives: family, neighbourhood, peer group, travel and school. Power-marginalisation, therefore, ought not to be understood as signalling a stasis associated with material poverty, nor as necessarily entailing a lack of aspirational commitment, but as a fluid or liquid process in respect to how students work out viable educational pathways.

Student practices are made up of deeply dissonant transactions. They have to figure out ways of navigating multiple spaces with different conflictual routines, rituals and expectations. Carving out a productive educational path requires mobility, strategy, fortitude and intense habitus negotiation and adaptation. For example, Domingo-Salie's chapter discusses the fragile adaptation processes of students who move away from their working-class families to attend a school in an upper-middle-class part of the city. Rinquest's chapter illustrates how students splice together place-making practices in the informal spaces of their school to mitigate the spatial dissonance they experience as they move between home and school. Norodien-Fataar's and Daniels' chapters discuss the ways in which students adopt educational survival practices in the unsupportive social spaces of their educational institutions. The chapters by Sonamzi, Fillies, Cooper and Feldman carefully illustrate the enormous chasm between the rich intellectual and literary practices of students within their family, neighbourhood and popular social spaces on the one hand, and the institutional misrecognition of these practices by their schools on the other.

The aforementioned chapters exemplify the acute disjunction between the lives and intellectual processing of the students whose stories are discussed in *TEPP*. I argue that this disjunction is a consequence of their educational institutions' inability to recognise and productively work with their lifeworld identifications, knowledge and literacy practices, providing them with a platform to facilitate their educational becoming. This book is, therefore, an attempt to make their epistemic evolution (Barnett 2007), arising out of their educational practices across power-marginalised spaces, more visible as a way of challenging dominant educational imaginaries.

The struggle over educational recognition

Such a task requires an understanding of what I argue is the (mis)recognitive agency of students that dominates our educational imaginary. The fulcrum of the book is thus a concerted focus on students' pathways in respect of their institutions' misrecognition. It posits an argument for placing students' educational agency at the centre of transforming our educational discourses and practices. *Recognition* is presented as the conceptual pivot for bringing students' practices into view. The struggle for recognition has been the subject of a highly significant debate in political theory, especially that between political theorists, Nancy Fraser and Axel Honneth (1995). Both approach the idea of recognition from the perspective of social theory that aims to ground the normative political aspects of their work in a critical analysis of contemporary power relations (see Fataar 2018).[1] Their divergent views stem from a basic disagreement about how to characterise the dynamics of social and political conflict (McNay 2008:271).

At the core of their disagreement is Fraser's insistence that struggles for recognition, such as occur in identity politics, are analytically distinct from conflicts over redistribution, while for Honneth, all conflict is an expression of a fundamental struggle for recognition. Stressing a subjectivist approach, Honneth advances a view that gives analytical primacy to the suffering and emotional grounds of agency against what he calls narrowly instrumentalist conceptions that are prevalent in conventional sociological accounts of action. In contrast, Fraser criticises Honneth's notion as 'uncritically subjectivist', which Fraser believes cannot be taken as a reliable indicator of injustice as this reduces social oppression to psychological harm. Fraser's objectivist position "defines recognition not as a psychological injury but as 'status subordination' understood as institutionalized patterns of discrimination and value injury" (McNay 2008:271).

I am sympathetic towards Honneth's conception, especially his insistence that recognition originates in, and is experienced on, bodies and lives through the psychologies of those who are at the receiving end of institutional and systemic injustice. This insight allows for bringing the affective dimension of subjectivity into conceptual view by highlighting, for example, the emotional dimensions, such as psychological harm, which have been enunciated recently by students on South African university campuses. The narratives in *TEPP* are also replete with complex and jarring affective dimensions associated with the selected students' experiences in their harsh and exclusionary educational spaces. Honneth's perspective highlights the emotional grounds for acting, in particular on the experience of being disrespected, which he argues can become the "motivational impetus for a struggle for recognition" (1995:107).

However, drawing on McNay's (2008) account of this debate, I suggest that while the affective dimension of suffering can become the motivational grounds for collective resistance, it can only be galvanised if persons can articulate their grievances through shared interpretive frameworks. Thus, a recognition model of struggle would have to provide what McNay calls a 'semantic bridge' between personal and impersonal goals (2008:274). Fraser's objectivist account is correct in asserting the material and power dynamics that constitute oppression, in terms of which she favours concomitant materialist politics that target the unequal distribution of power in society and systemic and institutional inequality. However, as McNay (2008:272) explains, Fraser's

---

1   This discussion draws liberally on my discussion of recognition in education (see Fataar 2018, forthcoming).

> ... non-identarian rendering of recognition leads her to abandon an experiential perspective that is associated with the idea of identity. Lacking this perspective, she is unable to explain the emergence of agency and the ways in which the subjective and objective dimensions of oppression are related to each other.

It is this emergent agency of students that *TEPP* attempts to give conceptual life to.

Students' recognitive agency in a 'decontainerised' nexus of relations

Working with Fraser's (2009) and Honneth's (1995) perspectives on recognition, I draw briefly on Bourdieu's notion of habitus to combine objectivist and subjectivist accounts of agency which provides me with a basis to bring the agency of university students into view. According to Bourdieu, the idea of habitus refers to a set of durably embodied social-epistemological dispositions that configure a subject's tendencies towards perception and action in the world, and confer a set of durable physical and psychological dispositions that define a subject's embodied being in the world. These dispositions are the result of the shaping force of power relations on the body, the incorporation of social structures into individual being (Bourdieu 1992). Bourdieu explains that the social agent is not an objective location within an abstract structure, as Fraser seems to insist, but as he explains, the agent is a mode of being in the world that is lived out in daily practices (Bourdieu 1979). McNay (2008:279) explains that Bourdieu's notion of habitus invokes:

> ... the way in which unique personal experiences are infused with regularity and uniformity insofar as they are the product of institutions. Immediate corporeal being contains within it the latent marks of abstract social structure. ... From the perspective of the habitus, emotions are not elemental or spontaneous givens, but are a type of social relation that are generated by and mediate the interactions between embodied subjects and social structures.

In this view of recognition, emotions emerge in and through practices that are significantly shaped by power relations that have been internalised through active engagement with these social-structural relations. Therefore, emotions are the product of practical social engagement with other individuals and social structures (McNay 2008:279). This creates what Bourdieu calls a "margin of freedom", which is a space for creative agency (2000:235). Human actors thus inevitably improvise new variations on logics of practice, which in tense conditions can rise to critical consciousness and concerted action in active engagements in their fields of practice, such as during schooling or university study. Thus, while the school or university's logic of power is based on the systemic misrecognition of those whom they educate, the students actively live, and may actively challenge, these systemic arrangements and work out a range of emergent practices through their daily educational engagements to open up new strategic possibilities in their education. Burkitt (1997:49) explains that because the contingency of human actions is patterned by power relations, such actions are never entirely random or autonomous. However, notwithstanding this, Bourdieu (1979) suggests that human action is never the final and fully determined product of structures. There is always a margin of freedom or a "space of possibles" for humans to construct, wherein they are capable of establishing "cognitive and motivating structures" (Bourdieu 1979:235) for augmented more-than-predisposed action in contingent contexts. It is within this "space of possibles" that students go about engaging educational institutions as field operators to work out a path of possibility in pursuit of their epistemic becoming.

Based on the discourse, I argue that this book makes visible key aspects of the recognition practices of students. Their recognition struggles consist of a series of subjective processes through which they encounter and navigate experiential circumstances and educational environments. They create survival-based educational pathways that involve subjective processes of coming to know and coming to be. For Barnett (2007), such coming to know "brings forth worthwhile attributes", in respect of which students' journey of coming to know is at least as important, if not more important, than the arrival (2007:433).

Understanding students' becoming as a journey involving subjective processes challenges the dominant view of education and learning as limited to classroom- or lecture-room-based cognitive processes. Such a view fails to account for learning as involving complex educational processes that are transacted in and across various lived spaces. Leander, Phillips and Taylor (2010:329) explain that this "classroom-as-container [view] … functions as an 'imagined geography' of education, constituting when and where researchers and teachers should expect learning to take place". As Leander *et al* (2010:330) suggest, learning is a process that crosses 'in school' and 'out-of-school' borders.

When viewed as a journey, students' educational becoming is more aptly understood in respect of how they traverse their various environments of, for example, their family, school, neighbourhood, university, lecture rooms, tutorial spaces and peer learning groups. In other words, educational becoming is transacted 'on the move' across multiple spaces (see Fataar 2015). Leander *et al* (2010:331) proffers this perspective by way of the following question:

> How are the dynamically moving elements of social systems and distributions, including people themselves and all manner of resources for learning as well, configured and reconfigured across space and time to create opportunities to learn?

A perspective on students' educational becoming as founded on a 'decontainerised' time-space nexus (Leander *et al* 2010:333) highlights the impact of political and sociocultural dynamics in an attempt to bring the impact of life outside school into account in our consideration of life inside their institution (Fataar 2015). The focus thus shifts to an understanding of students that stretches across their lived spaces. It concentrates on how the dynamics in these power-marginalised spaces position and inform their education, and how they go about developing their educational practices in respect of the affordances, through resources, discourses and tools, of their complex livelihoods.

The chapters

The focus of each chapter is on the active and flourishing expression of student practices and educational pathway construction. The educational field, institutional operations, curriculum knowledge selection processes and pedagogical orientations are the necessary background terrain for the students' educational lives. Each chapter thus discusses the multidimensional educational existence of the students.

Mobilising educational practices in and across power-marginalised spaces

The book is divided into three themes, each concentrating on core aspects of the overall focus. The first theme focuses on the interaction between students' lifeworlds and their educational practices in their out-of-school spaces, how they encounter these spaces as material surfaces, their uneven, thoroughly compressed and compromised nature, the poverty, hardship and informalised livelihoods, in light of high levels of anomie, unemployment, and tough domestic circumstances. It looks at how students live in these spaces in search of educational provenance, how they go about mobilising their resources and capitals to build their mediating agency to open for themselves a viable educational path.

Batandwa Sonamzi's chapter is based on research amongst four families living in a township. The focus is on how families in this power-marginalised space, contrary to popular perception, develop practices in their homes in support of their children's schooling. It illustrates how they accumulate capitals that support their children's education, challenging the assumption that township students come to school with cultural and educational deficiencies. The chapter challenges this discrepant view of township families and their children by offering an alternative reading of the domestic support practices that these families engage in, and the resources they draw on, to support their children's schooling.

Henry Fillies based his chapter on one year of ethnographic work among students in a rural township. Deep immersion in this township was central to this incisive analysis of the ways in which students develop learning practices that accumulate towards 'funding' their educational aspirations. He argues that their practices depend on their space-specific mediations in their family and neighbourhood and are crucial to the development of their learning practices. The chapter offers a discussion on how these young people read, think, strategise and build their learning practices as they interact with their surroundings. It shows how young people inhabit and interact with their social networks and relations in their mobilising of various 'funds of knowledge' in their community environs to develop their learning practices. Fillies develops an acute understanding of the meanings that young people construct for themselves in difficult times in order to make sense of their lifeworlds.

Young people's mobility from their neighbourhood into their schooling in dissonant middle-class terrain is the focus of Domingo-Salie's chapter. She presents a novel account of the ways in which students develop what she calls a 'trans-local' habitus as they encounter their school going between their power-marginalised home locations and their school experiences which they navigate on the basis of a spatial and class-cultural disconnect. The chapter focuses on the navigational practices of four historically disadvantaged students who accomplished their education 'on the move' between their working-class domestic environment and the dissonant terrain of a Focus School situated in a middle-class suburb. It discusses the practices that they employed in order to navigate the initially 'alien' terrain. Domingo-Salie opens a fascinating window into how students develop their pathways in respect of their spatial disconnect, and how they overcome this disconnect through identifying concerted activities, rules and routines that enable them to domesticate the school space in their building of viable futures.

Students' institutional pathway mediation in disjunctural educational spaces

This theme moves the book's focus into the educational institution. It builds on the previous theme's discussion of the students' mediating agency in the community context. Given the nature of their agency in the community context, as developed in the previous three chapters, here the focus is on how the students go about producing their mediating agency in light of the institutional materiality of their educational spaces.

The focus is on how the students live the deep unevenness of institutional spaces, how these spaces position them, and importantly, how they construct their practices. The focus is not per se on how institutions fall short on providing a supportive and inclusive institutional environment, but on how the students experience this environment, and how they go about producing their mediating agency in an attempt to bridge the gap. This theme focuses on how the students' epistemic becoming manifests in their institutional spaces.

Elzahn Rinquest offers an analysis of how a group of high school girls mediated the difficulties of belonging at a school. The research positioned her as an ethnographer in the girls' school environment in order to gain insight into how they lived and experienced their school-specific context. The chapter focuses on the informal out-of-classroom spaces of the school. It discusses how they interpreted and mediated their educational world and established their educational dispositions in their schooling terrain. Rinquest argues that their *desire to belong* is a key element to how they go about creating a 'place' for themselves at the school, partly as mitigation for their tough, alienating domestic lives. The school becomes a place for these girls where they make identifications that guide the way they see themselves. Rinquest argues that the girls interpreted the culture of the school, and acted in response to its discourses and their desire to belong, and that they consequently went on to construct very specific and stylised ways of being at the school.

Najwa Norodien-Fataar discusses the mediation practices of first generation disadvantaged students at a university. Based on qualitative work, she provides an account of the interaction between students' practices and the field conditions of their university. The chapter shows that the students' mediation practices were based on developing horizontal practices on the margins of the university field in order to address their alienation, from where they establish what she calls 'intersecting forms of engagements' that confronted the university field. Her core analytical conclusion is that the students build embodied learning practices (habitus) to establish their educational engagement at the university. This she uses to advance an account of what she terms the students' emergent 'logic of engagement' at the university, which, she argues, was constituted by the students' capacity to develop an emerging learning disposition that enabled them to adapt, shift and change their practices via encounters in a university environment that did not recognise their educational needs.

The chapter by Doria Daniels is based on the educational journeys of three students who accessed adult educational pathways after they were pushed out of their schools. The chapter discusses how their life contexts positioned and informed their educational trajectories, which provides the basis for a discussion of the students accessing 'second chance' adult education and training centres (AETCs) that provided them with 'triggers' for getting back on track to complete their schooling. This chapter brings into critical focus the role that their childhood contexts and histories played in their experiences with formal schooling. It explores how the AETCs served to restore trust in their capabilities and advance self-efficacy which, in effect, placed them as adults on a road of possibility. The chapter presents an analysis of these disenfranchised adults' educational journeys in respect of their childhood contexts, schooling experiences and their educational success at the AECTs.

Students' knowledge practices across disjuctural educational spaces

This is the culminating theme of the book. While the first two sections provide a view of the mediating student as productive, engaging, thinking and doing in and across power-marginalised spaces, this theme focuses explicitly on aspects of the students' knowledge and intellectualising practices. This section gives some idea about how they are thinking, processing and intellectualising in knowledge processes whether via their 'languaging' practices between school, popular culture and a media stage as discussed in Cooper's chapter or, in the case of school children, who mediate and establish learning practices in respect of attenuated justice-informed pedagogies of their teacher, as illustrated in Feldman's final chapter of the book. Both bring into view the students' humanness (which a deficit approach hides from view) as knowledge, literacy and language mobilisers. The normative purpose of this section is to advance a view of students as engaged and thinking beings, worthy of deep intellectual engagement via the formal registers and processes of schools and universities, for whom a rich curricular orientation would emphasise 'knowledge work for life use' and 'knowledge work' for exchange use.

Adam Cooper spent considerable time doing ethnographic work in an urban township. He focused on the language repertoires and practices of a group of students. His novel approach involved understanding their 'languaging' in three dissonant sites: their classroom, a radio programme space in which they participated, and language use in their rap group. Cooper discusses how their languaging in the three spaces worked via different linguistic and artistic expressions, how each space affectively and educationally positioned them in such a way that they each produced different linguistic registers. What is remarkable is that their language classes in the school 'traded' on the standard linguistic variety, which failed to recognise their intellectually meaningful language use in the other two out-of-school spaces. This lack of recognition of their linguistic varieties in the classroom space is borne out of a failure to provide a curriculum and pedagogical platform that would allow students to work with their own linguistic varieties and knowledges, on their own terms, and in rich interaction with school knowledge. This lack of pedagogical recognition is an example of a wider institutional and pedagogical misrecognition of the intellectual contributions that students are able to make to classroom learning.

In the final chapter of the book Jennifer Feldman takes up the challenge of establishing a platform for pedagogical recognition in her classroom engagement with students in a township school. Her chapter is a discussion of student learning dispositions within the context of a township primary school in the Western Cape. It is situated within the current South African schooling discourse and complexity of student learning in impoverished spaces and discusses how teachers and students, within a practice-based research process, came to mediate alternate learning practices. The chapter provides insight into the dynamics and complexity of student learning dispositions and school learning in impoverished spaces. It brings into view how teachers in a township school context adapted their pedagogies to mediate a more socially just approach to teaching and learning. Feldman considers ways in which the teachers could work with diverse cultural knowledges of their students to more deeply connect and engage them in the process. She discusses how the students' learning dispositions shifted and changed as the teachers, over time, came to adapt and enrich their modes of pedagogical transfer and student learning. The chapter concludes by discussing the potential for shifting or changing the 'terms of recognition' on which student learning is founded to engage with the meanings and values, the 'lived and feeling' aspects of students' learning dispositions, in order that school learning might resonate with the identities, knowledges, practices and literacies of all students.

In its entirety, the book works across the three sections to offer a view of students in their full existential dimensionality and crucially, as fully reflexive humans mediating the difficult materialities that position their mediating agency. Education processes ought to valorise and engage students in rich and complex learning processes to enable them to develop the capacity to establish meaningful and adaptive lives in a world dominated by brutal and troubling capitalising logics that cruelly exclude and alienate them (Zipin 2015). This book is, therefore, an attempt to provide understanding of and insight into the ways in which educational institutions misrecognise their students and fail to provide them an engaging educational platform to become productive critical citizens. A fully recognitive education orientation ought to be founded on an awareness of the educational practices and pathways of students in respect of South Africa's power-marginalisation. It would go on to provide an institutional and curricular orientation that valorises the complex knowledge work and intellectual processing that they produce to mitigate their own power-marginalisation and thereby go on to establish viable futures.

References

Barnett R. 2009. Knowing and becoming in higher education. *Studies in Higher Education*, 34(4):429–440. https://doi.org/10.1080/03075070902771978

Burkitt I. 1997. Social relationships with emotions. *Sociology*, 31(1):37–55. https://doi.org/10.1177/0038038597031001004

Bourdieu P. 1977. *Outline of a Theory of Practice*. Cambridge: Cambridge University Press. https://doi.org/10.1017/CBO9780511812507

Bourdieu P. 1979. *Distinction: A social critique of the judgement of social taste*. London: Routledge.

Bourdieu P. 1992. *An invitation to reflexive sociology*. Cambridge: Polity Press.

Bourdieu P. 2000. *Pascalian Meditations*. Cambridge: Polity Press.

Fataar A. 2015. *Engaging educational subjectivities across post-apartheid urban spaces*. Stellenbosch: AFRICAN SUN MeDIA. https://doi.org/10.18820/9781920689834

Fataar A. 2018. Placing students at the centre of the decolonising education imperative: Engaging the (mis)recognition struggles of students at the post-apartheid university. *Educational Studies*. (forthcoming)

Fraser N. 2009. *Scales of justice: Reimagining political space in a globalizing world*. New York: Columbia University Press.

Honneth A. 1995. *The struggle for recognition: The moral grammar of social conflicts*. Cambridge: Polity Press.

Leander K, Phillips N & Taylor K. 2010. The changing social spaces of learning: Mapping new identities. *Review of Research in Education*, 34:329–394. https://doi.org/10.3102/0091732X09358129

McNay L. 2008. The trouble with recognition: subjectivity, suffering and agency. *Sociological Theory*, 26(3):271–296. https://doi.org/10.1111/j.1467-9558.2008.00329.x

Yosso T. 2005. Whose culture has capital? A critical race theory discussion of community cultural wealth. *Race, Ethnicity and Education*, 8(1):69–91. https://doi.org/10.1080/1361332052000341006

Zipin L. 2015. Chasing curricular justice: How ethical vexations of redistributing cultural capital bring dialectics to the door of aporia. *Southern African Review of Education*, 21(2):91–109.

Zipin L, Sellar S, Brennan M & Gale T. 2015. Educating for Futures in Marginalized Regions: A sociological framework for rethinking and researching aspiration. *Educational Philosophy and Theory*, 47(3):227–246. https://doi.org/10.1080/001318 57.2013.839376

Chapter 2

Mobilising community cultural wealth: The domestic support practices of township families in support of their children's education

Batandwa Sonamzi

This chapter is based on qualitative research conducted amongst four families living in a township in the Western Cape, which I have called by the pseudonym, Duduza Extension. The chapter discusses how selected township families mobilise a range of networks and resources to support their children's schooling. I address a gap in the literature as identified by Miller, Pinderhughes, Young and Ferguson (2002) who point out that much research has focused on the negative issues that affect the academic outcomes of children living in impoverished circumstances, but that little research has been done on the domestic practices that support students in their school learning. In this respect, Lareau and Goyette (2014) observe that few studies have examined the dynamics within the home and therefore not much is known about how family life supports children's school learning. This chapter addresses this lacuna by providing an account of the support practices of impoverished families in their attempt to augment their children's schooling.

Methodologically, the chapter is based on qualitative research that "uses a naturalist approach that seeks to understand phenomena in context-specific settings" (Golafshani 2003:601). This approach allowed me to develop an interpretation of the families' support practices based on data obtained from semi-structured interviews and observations done in the homes of the four selected families. Informed by the theories of Bourdieu (1990) and Yosso (2005), the chapter presents an analysis of their domestic practices in light of their living circumstances in this township. The next section presents the theoretical lens that I used to understand how the domestic practices of the four township families supported their children's schooling.

Theoretical framework

Bourdieu describes capital as the accumulation of knowledge, skills and learning that advantages an individual and gives them a higher status in society (Bourdieu 1990:138). Cultural capital is acquired over time from the social origin of parents and families who pass on values, class-based practices and their social positions. According to Lareau (2000), Bourdieu's empirical work on cultural capital suggests that racial, ethnic, or linguistic minority students and their families may lack cultural capital or knowledge of how certain educational processes occur, which tends to present a deficit reading of the educational attainment of working-class and impoverished students. In contrast, I draw on Yosso's (2005) concept of CCW which extends Bourdieu's concept of cultural capital. I do this in order to show how the four families on whom this chapter is based supported their children's schooling. Yosso (2005) argues that cultural capital is not just inherited or possessed by the middle class. According to her, poor and marginalised communities also accumulate different forms of knowledge, skills, resources and abilities, what she calls community cultural wealth (CCW), which they use in their daily practices. Yosso defines CCW as the "accumulated assets and resources found in the lives and histories of disadvantaged students" (2005:77). She suggests that forms of capital from impoverished communities – namely, aspirational, linguistic, familial, social, navigational and resistant capital – are pivotal in providing the necessary support for children in their schooling practices.

Yosso's (2005) CCW model thus provides an alternative framework that critiques dominant discourses which assume that working class students have cultural deficiencies. She challenges such a view by highlighting aspects in poor communities which often go unacknowledged or unrecognised. Hence, in contrast to an educational system that sees working-class students as being deficient and lacking critical knowledge, Yosso posits working-class families and communities too as holders and creators of knowledge. I use Yosso's (2005) notion of CCW to describe the forms of capital that are nurtured in impoverished families and that provide support for their children's education. The chapter makes use of a narrative approach to present the data based on the lived experiences and practices of the four families' support of their children's schooling. In the next section I describe the township living circumstances of the four selected families.

The four families' complex living circumstances in a township context

The living circumstances of Duduza Township positions the four families, which are the focus of this study, in very particular ways. The township has a population of 45 000 with 10 520 households (Statistics South Africa 2011). The smaller area of Duduza Extension, the area where the four families currently live, was established in 2004 as part of the Reconstruction and Development Programme (RDP) housing to accommodate families from nearby informal settlements. The beneficiaries of the houses in Duduza Extension were coloured and black African families who were either unemployed or earning less than R3 500 per month. The RDP houses that they were given have basic facilities such as electricity, sanitation and water. Duduza Extension is one of six other areas, each of which has approximately 3 000 houses, which make up Duduza Township.

Many of the families in Duduza consist of large extended families living together. The houses in this area are RDP houses which comprise of 25 square metres of living space. These small homes consist of two bedrooms, an open-plan lounge and kitchen area, and a bathroom which includes a toilet. Those who can afford it, extend their house by adding on extra rooms to the existing brick building, or by adding a 'wendy house' (a small wooden structure) or shack dwelling at the back of the house which they then rent out for extra income.

Duduza can be described as an impoverished township environment with a myriad of social issues that impact directly on the children and youth of the area. These social dynamics, which can be attributed in part to the overpopulation and unemployment in this township, provide a fairly unstable living environment and include a high crime rate, extensive poverty, the lure of drugs, violence, gangs and school drop-out, to name but a few. Many families do not enjoy formal employment and the unemployment rate in this area in 2011 was 37.9% (Statistics South Africa 2011). Many families survive through informal small businesses like informal shops, braaing (barbequing) and selling meat on the pavements, as well as the informal hawking of fruit and vegetables, sweets and chips. Others survive through illegal activities that include selling drugs, the running of shebeens (informal bars) and other illicit activity.

To some extent Duduza is cut off from the surrounding areas. Transport in this area is difficult as there are no trains that run to the township. Families who were relocated here find this problematic as the area in which they were previously living was on a main train line. The population of Duduza and Duduza Extension therefore have to rely on buses and taxis which are more expensive. This has been an ongoing issue which is constantly raised by the community who are already struggling to afford basic living expenses. The families in Duduza find themselves having to spend significantly more money on transport if they work in areas outside of the township. This area also does not have a shopping mall or any small clustering of shops. This means that the population of Duduza needs to travel outside of the area to access banks, larger shops and other facilities, which in turn costs money. Families are therefore constrained by what is available to them within the township and most children attend their closest school as they have to walk daily to and from school. The average distance that children walk to school can be between 2 and 4 kilometres.

Lizo's family has lived in Duduza Extension for 3 years. Lizo's parents are married and living together with their four children. Lizo is 13 years old, in Grade 7 at one of the local township schools and is the third child in the family. Lizo's mother is unemployed and stays home. Her highest qualification is Grade 11. Lizo's father dropped out of school at the end of Grade 11. However, he later went back to school to complete Grade 12. He was unable to study further as he needed to start working to provide an income to support his family. He currently works for a construction company on a contract basis earning R2 500 per month and is the sole breadwinner in the family. The family is dependent on child social grants which they receive for all four children and which provide an additional income of R1 200 per month.

Duma's family is originally from Guguletu in the Cape Flats. Guguletu is considered a formal housing settlement in that it was a planned housing development. The formal housing within Guguletu, however, also contains informal backyard dwelling structures which individuals or families rent from the owners of the formal houses. It was in one of these backyard informal dwelling structures that Duma's family lived before moving to Duduza Extension. At that stage Duma's father was unemployed and therefore was eligible to register with the city of Cape Town's Department of Housing to apply for a RDP house in Duduza Extension.

Duma's parents divorced five years ago and Duma remained living with his father in the RDP house in Duduza Extension. His mother stays with relatives in the same area and Duma visits her regularly. Duma's father later remarried and his stepmother and their five-year-old son live together with Duma and Duma's cousin, who is 17 years old and completing Grade 11 at one of the local schools in the area. His cousin assists him with his homework.

Duma's father currently works at a newspaper company in Cape Town (which is approximately 30 km from Duduza Extension) as a packer and distributer. He takes two taxis to get from Duduza Extension to his place of work in Cape Town. This is both a costly and time-consuming arrangement and he leaves the house at approximately five o' clock in the morning to arrive at work on time. Duma's stepmother works as a cashier at a local supermarket chain store in an area approximately 15 km from where the family stays. She works a full day, leaving early in the morning and arriving home late in the evening. During his spare time and over weekends, Duma's father runs a small business to supplement his wages from his job at the newspaper company. He owns an industrial cutting machine (such as is found in butcher shops) which he uses to cut up sheep that have been slaughtered for events in the township.

Phelo lives with his parents who are married with three children. They live in an RDP house in Duduza Extension. Phelo is the second eldest and is 13 years old. He has a brother in high school who is 16 and a younger sister who is 5 years old. His sister should be in pre-school but the family does not have enough money to send her to school and so she stays at home with her mother during the day.

Phelo's father is the breadwinner in the family. He works for a company as a security guard and is sent to different locations, working the night shift. He earns approximately R3 000 per month. Phelo's mother stays at home and sews clothes which she sells to earn a small income to supplement her husband's salary. The family relies on the children's social grants to support the financial needs of the family.

Neither of the parents completed primary school, are unable to read or write in English, and therefore cannot assist Phelo with his school work. Phelo's father does however state that he supports his son's schooling by checking daily that Phelo has completed his homework before he allows him to socialise with his friends. Phelo's father says that Phelo is very self-motivated and will go to his room and complete his homework on his own without being reminded.

Lizel stays with her mother and younger sister. Lizel's mother was 18 years old when Lizel was born. She had to drop out of school before completing Grade 12 but went back the following year to complete her Grade 12 certificate. Lizel's father has not been involved in Lizel's life at all as he was arrested shortly after she was born and is serving a 35-year sentence in prison for armed robbery.

Lizel's mother is currently unemployed. Since leaving school she has had temporary work as a domestic cleaner and a shop cashier. The only income the family has is from the children's social grants and any temporary work that Lizel's mother is able to secure from time to time. A local minister and his wife have been involved in supporting this family for over a year. Lizel's mother says that the minister and his wife often stay with them in the house and cook and provide food for the family. The minister has continued to visit the father in prison and encourages Lizel's mother and the children to stay in contact with their father while he is in prison.

The discussion above provides the material contextual location in respect of which the four selected families support their children's schooling. It indicates the precariousness of their domestic environment. The next section is a discussion of the domestic practices of the four families which are the focus of the study that informed this chapter. In this section I bring into view the complex ways in which the domestic practices of these four families, living within the constraints of the social conditions described above, support their children's education.

The accumulation of cultural capital that supports students' successful learning in a township context

According to Yosso (2005:79), familial capital refers to cultural knowledge that is developed among family members – siblings, aunts, uncles, friends and grandparents – that carry a sense of community history, memory and cultural consciousness. Familial capital can be seen as a cultural resource that is nurtured by, and within, one's family. This form of cultural capital highlights the role that the immediate and extended family members play in supporting their children's school learning.

Ngwaru (2012) states that children who form constructive relationships with parents and other family members early on in their lives are more likely to build social competency and good peer relationships outside the home environment. This form of social development assists the children to adequately express emotion, desire, needs, consider the feelings of others, express their viewpoint and listen to the viewpoints expressed by others (Ngwaru 2012). Families in this study provided emotional support for their children and built constructive family relationships by spending time together in the home and doing things together as a family. Lizo's grandmother spent time with the children by telling them stories about their family history. This storytelling, as a form of familial support, provided the children with an oral history of the family and an understanding of the parents' and grandparents' struggles to provide support for their children. The parents felt that it was these stories about the family history that encouraged their children to study hard at school and get a good education so that they may have good job prospects in the future.

Familial support includes support from extended family members who provide additional emotional support and encouragement, and who also financially provide for the children by paying for them to go on additional educational excursions offered by the school. Cousins of the families, for example, made it their mission to follow up on the academic progress of the students and buy them gifts as a way of motivating them to work hard and pass. This practice, according to the parents, assisted to keep the students focused on their school work.

Family support practices were also evident in the way in which the parents and other siblings supported the students with homework. While many of the parents were not at home during the day due to long working hours, all of the families discussed how they ensured that their children had an adequate work space where they could complete their homework. All the families lived in small and often cramped living conditions, yet had prioritised space in the home with a desk where their children could complete their homework and study for exams.

Lizo's mother was supportive of the homework study group that Lizo and his friends established. She showed a keen interest in assisting the students in their work by attending Saturday mathematics classes at the school as this enabled her to help her children with their school work. Although Lizo and his friends prefer that his father provides support with the mathematics homework his mother notes:

> I know it's because I'm not good at maths. But I don't worry about that, I support the group and just laugh at them. I decided to attend Saturday maths classes with him [Lizo], so that I can be capacitated to help him.
>
> (Lizo's mother)

Besides directly involving themselves in their children's school learning, the families also discussed how they attempted to build strong family relationships which encouraged their children to stay indoors and away from the negative influences of township life. The families described how they spent recreational time together. For instance, Duma's parents go to movies together as a family and sometimes eat out at restaurants. Duma and his father also spend time together fixing his father's old car or watching sport on television. Other families stated that they encouraged their children to stay home to avoid bad influences and dangers associated with other young people in the township.

Social capital refers to the network of people and community resources that provide poor families with the ability to draw on social relationships, interactions and networks (Yosso 2005). Social capital can be considered a cultural resource that families in townships draw on, as well as an asset that supports impoverished families in their daily lives. Singh, Mbokodi and Msila (2004) report that many parents do not see their role as engaging in the school learning practices of their children as they believe that the school is competent enough to deal with their children. The parents in my study spoke passionately about wanting to be involved in social and school networks that support their children's learning. What my study highlights is that while parents' work situations or educational level may limit their involvement in school activities or assisting their child to complete homework tasks, the parents are able to draw on other family members or members of the community to assist them to support their children's school learning. An example of this was Lizel's mother's involvement in the church. It was through her involvement in the church that she found out about a Further Education and Training (FET) college where she later enrolled to study further. As a result, Lizel's mother says that her daughter sees her as a role model which encourages her to commit to working harder at school.

The three boys and their families in the study are members of local soccer clubs. The parents discussed how they actively support their children's involvement in the sport clubs as it keeps them away from the negative influences of the township and encourages them to dream of one day becoming successful soccer players. According to the families, involvement in the soccer club creates a form of discipline for their children as being part of a club and playing in a team requires them to obey the rules of the club and commit to attending practices if they want to play in the team matches. The parents show their support by making time to go and watch their children play their soccer matches.

Another form of social support that assisted to build cultural capital to support the students' school learning was the access to a mathematics tutor organised by the school. All four families prioritised finances to pay for the mathematics tutoring provided by the school. They send their children to school on Saturdays for two hours at the cost of R100 every month for their children to receive extra support in mathematics. The school also provides adult mathematics classes which some of the parents attend in order to support their children's maths homework from school.

For Yosso (2005), linguistic capital refers to the intellectual and social skills attained through communication experiences in more than one language. Linguistic capital, as a resource, highlights the possibility that working-class students arrive at school with multiple language and communication skills from their homes and communities. An example of linguistic capital is found in township family environments through the rich storytelling traditions that include listening to and recounting oral histories, parables, stories and proverbs. The study's findings showed that the families spent time talking with each other and sharing stories passed down from the parents' childhood or stories about extended family members. This form of linguistic capital not only gives them knowledge about the history of the family, but also builds their communication and language skills.

A further example of how the diverse cultural and linguistic environments found in the township context can support school learning is seen in friendships which township students establish across cultural and language divides. Liou, Antrop-Gonzalez and Cooper's (2009) research suggests that many high-achieving students seek friends who possess diverse cultural and linguistic backgrounds because they positively support their academic achievement. An example of this is a friendship that Lizo developed with a classmate. As his friend was not proficient in either isiXhosa or Afrikaans, the boys had to communicate in English. This developed Lizo's acquisition of spoken English which, in turn, supported his school learning which takes place only in English.

The families in the study also supported their children's literacies through their interaction with English programmes on television. All of the families interviewed made mention of how they actively encouraged their children to watch English programmes on TV and spent time afterwards discussing and debating aspects of the programmes with their children. One of the fathers noted that "these debates give the children the foundation to use to help them when they have an argument at school".

Other support practices that the families engaged in, which supported their children's linguistic ability, involved buying English educational games and books. Duma's father says that he spends time reading to his children to develop their love for reading. Other families bought English music CDs or DVDs. All the parents showed an awareness that they needed to develop and build their children's competency in English in order for their children to be successful in their school learning. Phelo's father notes:

> You need to take your child to places where they can hear and use English – for example church, clubs and library. You must make sure that the children's play areas and toys include materials in English and also encouraging your child to watch and listen to programmes on television, radio and the internet where they will hear English.

What is apparent from the above discussion is that despite impoverished families being seen as not actively supporting their children's linguistic competency, the families in the study, despite the constraints of their social circumstances, both valued linguistic competency and supported their children's English language development in various ways. All four families made an effort to provide their children with multiple opportunities to engage in the building of linguistic competency so that they might achieve in their school learning and aspire to studying further after school in order to establish a successful career path.

Yosso (2005:77) describes aspirational capital as the ability of students to maintain hopes and dreams for the future even in the face of real and perceived barriers. This is evidenced in those who allow themselves and their children to dream of possibilities beyond their present circumstances, often without the objective means to attain those goals. Thus, aspirational capital, as a form of resiliency, can be described as a cultural resource which is acquired through parents and families as a way to transmit attitudes that are needed to succeed despite the families' impoverished living circumstances.

Agulana (1999, in Alika & Endosa 2012:256) state that the family lays the foundation for the psychological, moral, spiritual and learning dispositions of their children. Olivier (2006) notes that children imitate the behaviour of 'significant others' within their immediate environments, thereby suggesting that parents, peers and other community members play a powerful role in motivating children in their learning. Parents' perceptions of their children's abilities and support, in their sense of efficacy and aspirations of success, therefore play an important motivating role in their children's learning (Olivier 2006:56).

The participants in the research consistently referred to motivating their children as a way of supporting them to believe in their abilities so that they could perform well at school and become successful in their lives. The families displayed high expectations for their children and believed that they could flourish and achieve in their schooling. The parents described how they used their own life stories to motivate their children to attend and stay at school. These stories included their own struggles associated with their upbringing as well as discussions as to why they did not finish school. Linked with this was the evidence that without sufficient education, they as parents had been unable to secure employment that could provide financially for the family to move out of poverty:

> I always tell my children that without education you won't get a nice job like my late brother who was a lawyer and I tell them about my cousins who have well-paying jobs. Education is very important today.   (Parent)

It is these stories and constant reminders by the parents that they believe have motivated their children to focus on their studies and achieve at school in order that they may have the opportunity to study further and have well-paid jobs that will enable them to change their living circumstances. The discussion the families had with their children about the importance of performing well in school placed an emphasis on education as a means to escape poverty. The parents reiterate that having good marks might enable them to receive a bursary that will help exempt their already struggling families from paying for their education. The four students have dreams of becoming a doctor, engineer, lawyer and fashion designer. The parents believe that it is their responsibility to keep this focus and dream alive as it assists their children to see beyond their immediate circumstances and aspire to a different future.

A further motivation by the parents in the study was their constant references to other successful family members who grew up in impoverished families but, through hard work and further studies, managed to get out of poverty:

> I tell him about my cousins who are having well-paying jobs and nice cars, that they persevered at school under difficult conditions, their mother being single managed to take them to school. Fortunately they got bursaries and worked hard to pass. Look where are they today.   (Lizo's father)

These family members were not only held in high esteem by the parents and the students, but were regularly invited to visit the family and speak to the students about how they worked hard at school in order to achieve the marks that would allow them to enrol in university studies and get a good job. Ongoing contact with these successful family members provided aspirational support that helped their children to believe in themselves and look up to their extended family members as role models and people who have become successful in life.

The data discussed in this section highlights how the domestic support practices of the families provided forms of capitals that supported the four students in their school learning. Despite the impoverished living conditions of the four families, they still have high hopes and dreams for their children's future-*aspirational capital*, which they support in numerous ways through their everyday living within the family, extended family and community-*social capital*. The families use the available resources to support the acquisition of language-*linguistic capital* and they use their life histories to motivate their children to stay in school and be successful in their learning-*familial capital*. It is in this way, through the mobilisation of these forms of capitals, that the families in this study provided cultural capital that supported their children's schooling.

Conclusion

Drawing on Yosso's (2005:77) alternative understanding of forms of capitals as "accumulated assets and resources found in the lives and histories of disadvantaged students" the chapter has presented an account of how the four families' domestic practices in an impoverished township context have provided support for their children's schooling. These practices demonstrated how the families mobilised various forms of capitals in their families and communities that enabled their children to achieve at school. This chapter has presented an alternative view of township living and families' domestic support practices to show that families living in impoverished circumstances possess and utilise an array of knowledge, skills, abilities and contacts that support and build capital for their children's schooling. It has highlighted that families living in impoverished circumstances, contrary to the perceptions of many, value their children's education and have high educational aspirations for their children. This is consistent with the normative justice seeking approach of the book that presents underprivileged students as flourishing, thinking, talking, creating, intellectualising and knowledge generating, which the book places on the table theoretically as a way of shifting the conversation towards their fuller educational recognition.

References

Alika H & Edosa O. 2012. Relationship between broken homes and academic achievement of secondary school students in Oredo local government area of Edo State, Nigeria. *College Student Journal*, 256–263.

Bourdieu P. 1990. *In other words: Essays towards a reflexive sociology*. Stanford: Stanford University Press.

Epstein J. 2001. *School, family, and community partnerships: Preparing educators and improving schools*. New York: Westview Press.

Golafshani N. 2003. Understanding Reliability and Validity in Qualitative Research. *The qualitative Report*, 8(3):597–607.

Lareau A. 2000. Contours of Childhood: Social Class Differences in Children's Daily Lives. *Berkeley Collection of Working and Occasional Papers*, (1):39.

Lareau A & Goyette K (eds). 2014. *Choosing homes, choosing schools*. Russell Sage Foundation.

Liou DD, Antrop-Gonzalez R & Cooper R. 2009. Unveiling the promise of community cultural wealth to sustaining Latino students' college going information networks. *Educational Studies*, 45(6):534–555. https://doi.org/10.1080/00131940903311347

Miller D, Pinderhughes E, Young N & Ferguson C. 2002. Family composition and circumstance: Forster care. *Encyclopaedia of Education*, 807–820.

Ngwaru J. 2012. Parental involvement in early childhood care and education: Promoting children's sustainable access to early schooling through social-emotional and literacy development. *Southern African Review of Education*, 18(2):25–40.

Olivier M. 2006. The impact of deprived environments on learner motivation. *Africa Education Review*, 3(1 & 2):48–66. https://doi.org/10.1080/18146620608540442

Singh P, Mbokodi S & Msila V. 2004. Black parental involvement in education. *South African Journal of Education*, 24(4):01–307.

Statistics South Africa. 2011. http://www.statssa.gov.za

Yosso TJ. 2005. Whose culture has capital? A critical race theory discussion of community cultural wealth. *Race, Ethnicity and Education*, 8(1):69–91. https://doi.org/10.1080/1361332052000341006

Chapter 3

Young people's learning practices within a rural working-class context

Henry Fillies

Introduction

The construction of students' learning practices in relation to their educational aspirations in their neighbourhood context is a complex process that largely depends on their context-specific mediations. This chapter focuses on the learning practice formation of young people within a rural working-class context and examines how they go about developing these practices within their everyday lived experiences. It is my view that what these students do and their interactions on a daily basis contribute to their development of scripts (or ways of doing things) and strategies (tools to overcome obstacles) in order to deal with challenges. What this chapter offers is a discussion on how these young people think and interact with their learning in relation to their aspirations. Based on an ethnographic approach, this chapter analyses the learning practice formation of high school students in a poor rural community outside Cape Town. I utilised participant observation as well as unstructured and semi-structured interviews to gather in-depth qualitative data with the purpose of illustrating the complexity of young peoples' learning practice formations.

Drawing conceptually on the works of Pierre Bourdieu and authors in the funds of knowledge tradition (González, Moll, Floyd-Tenery, Rivera, Rendon, Gonzales & Amanti 1995), this chapter emphasises the complex relationships between the sociocultural background and lived experiences that make up students and families' dispositions towards education. I argue that the manner in which these young people inhabit and interact with their social spaces, as determined by the particular networks, movements and practices that they mobilise in those spaces, provides the mediating text in terms of which they construct their learning practices. I will also show how these rural youth mobilise various funds of knowledge to develop their learning practices. I have two broad objectives with this chapter: The first is to show how five students who are exposed to socioeconomic challenges perceive, acquire and utilise their different funds of knowledge. The second is to argue that, based on their funds of knowledge, these students construct learning practices that succeed in opening up a productive educational path for them. My overall aim is to provide an understanding of the construction of the learning practices of young people in their neighbourhood context which involves complex processes of struggle, resistance and mediation.

Academic research on education in a rural community context in South Africa is fairly scant, particularly with regard to the construction of working-class students' learning practices. In most instances various aspects of education are explored in isolation from community influences. This chapter grapples with the question: What role do community influences play in shaping working-class students' learning practices? In doing so, I attempt to understand what social meaning young people construct for themselves in difficult times, and how they make sense of their world and their experiences in the world in relation to their learning practices.

In today's education climate, students, families and communities are often described from a deficit perspective. This perspective supports the view that working-class communities lack assets for learning. In my opinion, this perspective fails to understand that there is more to working-class students, families and communities than the range of difficulties they face; they do also have access to resources that provide assets for learning. In order to shift this deficit perspective, educators should regard families as sources of learning and focus on the strengths and resources that students bring to the classroom. Put simply, "the educational process can be greatly enhanced when teachers learn about their students' everyday lives" (Gonzales, Moll, Floyd-Tenery, Rivera, Rendon, Gonzales & Amanti 1995:6).

What I will seek to highlight is the complex relationship between the sociocultural background and the lived experiences of young people, as well as their families' attitudes towards education. I aim to argue that these students' experiences and interaction with their social settings are defined by the specific networks and practices they mobilise within those settings, which in turn affects the way in which they build their learning practices. By combining the arguments of Bourdieu and Moll, Amanti, Neff, and Gonzáles, we may find social, economic and cultural circumstances that compel students to develop alternative responses to learning opportunities. I will further attempt to establish a so-called 'think piece' on the construction of students' learning practices in the context of their neighbourhoods, which involves complex processes of mediation.

In her work *Steering by the Stars: Being Young in South Africa*, Ramphela (2002) offers a poignant account of teenagers struggling to fulfil their ambitions in challenging circumstances. Her study centres on young people's choices and how the consequences of those choices unfold in their lives. From the students' actions, she gleans their understanding of the world, thereby providing us with insight into all the factors at play in their lives and, thus, their learning. Every day, I encounter youth who struggle to cope with the demands of everyday life. Many of them are confronted with poverty on a daily basis and experience the burden of their circumstances through the eyes of the local community and outsiders. These aspects influence their self-concept as well as their future ambitions. This has led me to explore working-class students' conceptualisation of their learning experiences outside school. This discussion is essential, as it provides the framework within which the study should be understood. I offer a description of how social matters affect students' conceptualisation of their learning practices. It also provides insight into the way in which the students' material circumstances in their neighbourhoods define and influence their learning practices in their spatial context. Uniquely, therefore, this chapter seeks to illustrate the meaning of these young peoples' learning experiences in relation to their various everyday lived realities and their interaction with their cultural setting in constructing their learning practices.

This analysis of students' experiences in relation to their social setting is intended to fill a gap in the current literature. Firstly, the chapter explores a fairly under-researched community, namely those in a rural setting. Secondly, from a theoretical standpoint, the study provides a deeper understanding of learning practice formation among youth in a working-class context. From a sociological perspective, this study focuses on the way in which high school students in a rural working-class neighbourhood build their learning practices within their specific community dynamics. I will argue that young peoples' formation of learning practices is influenced by their involvement in various institutions and exposure to various cultural resources. Extensive studies on learning in a South African context have thus far revealed many significant factors about learning and the way in which working-class students' culture, context and learning are intertwined with their everyday school life. While these studies have offered important findings, they have, however, failed to describe a deeper understanding of how working-class students build a range of learning practices based on their interaction with their environment. I find this lack of understanding conceptually troubling in the sense that it contributes little to our notion of the multifaceted interrelationship between cultural resources and learning. It is also problematic because it limits our ability to better support rural working-class students to achieve positive schooling outcomes.

Defining learning practice formation has never been easy. Doing so in the context of working-class youth is even more challenging (see Fataar & Du Plooy 2012). This is due to the fact that these young people construct their lives across various spaces, and position themselves within the sociocultural, economic and political realities of those spaces. The literature mostly defines learning practice formation as a process that occurs through and by means of young people's everyday activities, and is maintained by multiple interlinked social, economic and political relationships that tie their communities together and create social fields that transcend boundaries. Yet, this definition of learning practice formation has been criticised for failing to answer certain questions, such as the type of community it relates to, its limitations, and the type of practices it includes (Fataar 2015).

The analytical task in this chapter is to illustrate how the students define and understand their learning practices and mediate them within their physical context, which later contributes to their learning practice formation. This discussion will inter alia show that the students' learning experiences, learning practices and life trajectories in the community are linked to and stem from what occurs and is learnt in their neighbourhoods. I will therefore establish new ways of explaining how poor students construct their learning practices against the backdrop of their neighbourhoods.

The study was conducted within the qualitative interpretative paradigm. I seek to describe and understand how these students, (un)intentionally and through their mediations within their lived realities, engage with their funds of knowledge to form their learning practices. Qualitative research tools such as field notes, participant and non-participant observations as well as formal and informal interviews were employed to answer the research question and achieve the study objectives. My findings indicate that in achieving learning objectives against multiple community backgrounds, students position themselves in relation to various funds of knowledge. I will now proceed to discuss the theoretical approach that I used to analyse my data.

Theoretical considerations

My conceptual focus combines (i) the sociological concepts of Bourdieu (1977, 1986, 2006), including doxa, habitus, field and capital, and (ii) the funds of knowledge approach proposed by Moll, Amanti, Neff and González (1992). This combination enables me to explore the link between these concepts and the focus of this chapter, namely how rural working-class students construct their learning practices based on either their notion of, or their engagement with, the material circumstances in their neighbourhood context. In my view, students' learning practices are formed within and across various connections, activities and orientations. These operate as "sets of multiple interlocking networks of social relationships through which ideas, practices, and resources are unequally exchanged, organized and transformed" (Levitt & Jaworsky 2007:132).

The studying of young people's learning practice formation thus far has been far too superficial. Most literature on this topic has failed to offer a complex understanding of how viable learning practices in relation to future aspirations are formed in everyday circumstances. Existing research has also not offered us an understanding of the resources and strategies that young people employ and the way in which they utilise their agency to maintain and sustain their learning practices. I believe that understanding the ways in which students move, mobilise networks, and build and utilise learning resources in the course of their everyday learning activities is a vital component of comprehending their learning practices.

The analytical focus of the study is the learning practices or, as Moll *et al* (1992) call them, the funds of knowledge that students identify with in their lived realities outside school. According to Moll *et al* funds of knowledge refers to the vital cultural practices and ways through which students obtain knowledge and information within households which they then use to survive or flourish (1992:21). The students in this study have a number of funds of knowledge in their lives, including, though not limited to, the following:

- Family funds (knowledge/skills/practices utilised in their family lives, including extended families)
- Community funds (knowledge/skills/practices utilised in the community, such as the understanding of community systems and social networks)
- Peer culture funds (knowledge/skills/practices utilised in their interactions with friends)
- Knowledge obtained through their interaction with the media (television, websites, social media, etc.)

It is against this backdrop that young people's learning practices should be understood as a complex combination of a range of sociocultural resources. These sociocultural resources include the family, community practices and their lived cultural agency as they experience it at any given time. My task is one of shedding light on how students adjust their perceptions and actions of learning, and adapt and build their learning practices within the context of their acute material circumstances.

Methodology

The data used in this chapter were derived from a broader study (Fillies 2015) on the social and educational experiences of South Africa's working-class youth in their rural communities. This was supplemented with participant observations and interviews during the 2013/2014 school year at Arendsehoop (pseudonym), a small township outside Stellenbosch. Note, however, that the study did not focus on the school itself, but rather on the lived circumstances around the school that informed the young peoples' learning practices.

Ethnographic methods were selected for this study in order to capture the participants' authentic voices. I sought to 'read' the smallest of details, such as the interactions and events that contributed to the students' learning practice formation. The reason for selecting ethnography as research method was twofold: (i) to describe and understand the students' social and cultural lives in their social and cultural worlds (the emic perspective), and (ii) to build on the details and understanding of the students' social and cultural worlds in order to develop a new sociocultural perspective (the etic perspective). My ethnographic research enabled me to understand the events in the context where they occurred (Neuman 2011). In fact, one of the most important objectives of the study was to gain an understanding of the context within which the students perceived their learning practices.

Focused semi-structured personal interviewing strategies were used in combination with careful observations to collect information. Students were asked to tell their own stories about their lived experiences so that each story could be related to their learning practices (González, Moll & Amanti 2005). In this way, local stories on what it takes to be a student in a working-class neighbourhood could be linked to the critical analysis of the students' learning practice formation.

Participants were selected through purposive sampling based on their willingness to take part in the study. All ethical considerations regarding research with students were adhered to and pseudonyms were used throughout (Clark 2008:14). The participants, Cherry, Sally, Tom, Ruby and Musa, were selected from two unstructured interviews with students who displayed a positive attitude towards their schooling and achieved excellent school results. They were also willing to freely share and describe their lived experiences in terms of their aspirations and desires. In addition, they were familiar with the neighbourhood dynamics and influences in the community that could potentially affect their learning practices. Like González, Moll and Amanti (2005), I utilised a combination of careful observations, open-ended questions and semi-structured interviewing strategies in an attempt to accurately reflect the complex functions of households against their sociocultural and socioeconomic backgrounds.

By drawing on the notion of funds of knowledge (González, Moll & Amanti 2005), the data were organised thematically. The questions put to the participants in order to obtain the data mainly centred on a description of their living conditions and their experiences thereof in constructing their learning practices. Questions also touched on practices in their households, peer groups and the media that served as sources of learning. The data enabled me to document the spatial context of the students, and their experience of how the spatial context of their working-class neighbourhood affected their learning practices. The following section contains a discussion of key aspects of these students' funds of knowledge, and how these contributed to the formation of their learning practices.

"It's about where you find yourself": student lives and the socio-spatial dynamics of Arendsehoop

This section focuses on the students' rural town context. I emphasise what González, Moll and Amanti (2005) call the "messiness of ordinary life" in the neighbourhood. 'Messiness' (González *et al* 2005) in this context refers to everyday activities. Arendsehoop is a disadvantaged rural community in the Western Cape Winelands district. The neighbourhood is characterised by extensive poverty and deep-rooted social challenges. The divide between the haves and the have-nots is clearly visible. This was also evident from the interviews, when one student said:

> When you look more closely at the nitty-gritty of things, everyone's got issues. They don't show it, but I can sense it. They [referring to the haves] think they are better than us. There are no jobs here, and very few opportunities for young people. (Sally)

Another student, Cherry, echoed this view. The eldest of three children, Cherry lives with her parents on a farm several kilometres from school. She shares a three-roomed house (a kitchen/lounge and two bedrooms) with her parents and her younger brother and sister. Upon entering the home, the large number of religious posters against the walls caught my eye. I immediately sensed that faith played an important part in this family's life. Everyone regularly attends church. The family is involved in religious activities, particularly on Sundays. Conditions on the farm are difficult. Cherry's father used to abuse alcohol, which caused the family financial difficulty. However, he learnt from his mistakes, decided to abstain from alcohol and has since become a teetotaller. By witnessing how her father coped with this difficult situation, Cherry learnt that she too could overcome obstacles in her life. She shared the following during an interview:

> I learnt from him not to make such a mistake in life. If I fall, I'm responsible to get up again and learn from it.

Her circumstances, therefore, offered her an opportunity to learn which made her "a stronger person". Her mother has to work on the farm in order for the family to retain their house. She is the family's primary breadwinner, while Cherry's father occasionally manages to secure work. However, the mother's income is not sufficient to supply all the household's needs. During one of our interviews, Cherry described their circumstances as follows:

> Things are terrible here. Poverty is a major problem. Believe me, it's one thing to describe it to you, but something completely different to actually experience it. It isn't easy. We receive money from a social grant, which isn't enough. As you know, this community's economy is bad. We simply struggle along on our own.

Her words gave me a true sense of their impoverished existence, especially the lack of basic resources needed for survival. Although these problems are clearly visible in the neighbourhood, there is little indication that something is being done to adequately address them. Various social organisations have attempted to offer programmes as part of a youth empowerment strategy, which does instil a sense of hope for the future in the residents of the neighbourhood. On the other hand, in line with Gibson's (1996:9) observations, they (the community) still expect government to provide them with housing of a reasonable quality, free water and electricity, fair treatment, financial assistance, transport, assistance in medical and other emergencies, as well as care for the aged.

The construction of the students' learning practices in their family context

The aim of this section is to present the way in which these students' circumstances inform and build their learning practices. The students' awareness of their social context is critically important for their academic journeys. Moreover, it is vital to understand how these students' circumstances inform their specific dispositions towards learning and education.

At the start of the interviews, I realised that these students struggled with a particularly challenging combination of needs on a daily basis. I soon discovered that the students' families played a vitally important part in their learning practice formation. It is within their family contexts that they were being taught how to understand their physical world.

The students' households seem to be literacy-rich environments. Cherry's mother is the forewoman at the farm's plant nursery. Due to her mother's involvement in growing flowers and plants, Cherry too has developed an extensive knowledge of farming activities. She had the following to say about her mother's function at the nursery:

> My mother knows everything that goes on in the [cultivating] tunnels [pointing to the place where plants and flowers are grown]. We supply Pick n Pay and Woolworths [both large retail chains]. The farmers [farm owners] ask her what to do.

The mother's knowledge of flowers and plants is invaluable, ranging from irrigation to more in-depth knowledge of agricultural equipment and land use. In a school setting, this knowledge would cover aspects such as the genetic modification of plants, or would be able to inform a study on the effects of insecticides on the ecosystem. She imparts this knowledge to Cherry and her other children who are also taught the economic implications should these plants be damaged. Both the economic and social value of these flowers and plants for the farming community is therefore highlighted. The fact that the students know the value attached to growing agricultural crops indicates that this household's funds of knowledge relate to culture, history, economics and science.

Cherry has utilised the funds of knowledge that she obtained through her parents' work on the farm to acquire valuable insight into agriculture. This knowledge has also equipped her with marketing and management skills, and exposed her to processes of global integration with an increased awareness of global agricultural trends due to the privatisation and mechanisation of neighbouring farms. Yet, she does not regard farm work as her profession of choice. In a sense, it has stimulated an awareness of her future professional status. Instead of becoming more confident in applying agricultural knowledge, she has increasingly started to withdraw from participating in farm work due to what she saw as farm labourers' straitened circumstances.

Ruby is another student with notable exposure to literacy practices at home. Her household has rich musical funds of knowledge which was plain to see during home visits. When I accompanied her out and about in the neighbourhood, she often carried her cellphone with her and sang along with the songs playing through her earphones. I established that the family loved karaoke – displaying lyrics on the TV screen with everyone lustily singing along. She told me: "We discuss our musical preferences. I love rhythm and blues or R&B as they call it, as well as classical music."

Through music, Ruby not only takes part in literacy practices such as reading lyrics and learning songs, but has also established connections between the contemporary musical culture in her neighbourhood and in other areas. These musical practices in Ruby's home have the potential to support her in achieving academic success. As a student, Ruby regards it as her responsibility to build social patterns of engagement through collaborative learning strategies in her community. This has made her more confident in her ability to manage her learning practices which was evident when she described her strengths as a student:

> I do my homework … learn through listening … work out questions to help me better understand the work. I always give it my best shot and do not get involved in negative things. I like reading, but I'm not really a good reader. I read whenever I get a chance. I also sometimes start reading a book, but don't finish it. If the children don't read, how will they understand the books they receive at school?

Ruby's words emphasise her diligence and commitment to her education. Perceptions of attending university are often shaped by these students' social networks and family funds of knowledge. In their families, thinking about education goes beyond the conventional ideas, beyond what everyone in the community expects the students to be. These working-class students are strongly encouraged to continue their education, which serves as sources of social and cultural capital on which they can draw. While this is a reality in working-class families I also observed how educational perspectives and practices sometimes take alternative forms. At times, these students struggle to make a connection between their everyday practices and their educational objectives.

In the evenings I also saw people gathering around the fire. I joined them on various occasions to escape the cold. I realised that this was a gathering place where the rich storytelling culture of the neighbourhood came to the fore. According to Mallan (1991 in Phillips 1999:3), storytelling is a social activity. These students told jokes, listened to others' stories, and thought up and told their own. It is in this space that Sally's literacy practices were influenced in her family context. Sally told us:

> I really enjoy storytelling. In the evenings, we huddle around the fire, and then my father tells us stories. He tells us stories about his young days and how things were then. Stories about the jackal and the wolf, ghost stories, sport stories, stories making the news, as well as stories about life. We joke around. You know, the things children enjoy. Also personal stories about his life experiences. We look at pictures and talk about them, and we're able to link many of the stories to our personal life experiences. I remember the stories, and when I go visit my friends or family at their homes, I retell them.

This storytelling culture complements who they are. It is presented in an enjoyable manner as a source of entertainment as well as to gain a better understanding of the world. In many households, storytelling is a dominant activity and is regarded as an important way in which children can learn, instilling in them good moral values, traditions and many other things. It also fosters a sense of closeness between parents and their children, as well as with the broader community. In addition, parents may use it as an opportunity to talk to their children about general matters, social challenges, and the moral and cultural values that society expects of them. This enables the students to create expectations of their own.

In this section, a few of the family funds of knowledge that these students rely on in order to construct their learning practices were discussed. The funds of knowledge within the family context are often freely shared with other children, thereby unintentionally expanding and defining their learning practices. Having had insight into the personal experiences in the student's homes, it became clear that they led their lives amidst a dynamic combination of behaviours, skills, interactions and values, which each family expressed in their own unique way. These funds of knowledge provide us with a better understanding of matters such as their choice of reading material, their interaction with their parents, the structuring of their learning activities, and the forging of strong family ties. Although the families all struggle financially, they do everything in their power to offer their children opportunities to learn. In many instances these funds of knowledge also tie in with what is happening in their community and with the existing community knowledge base, which is an aspect I will turn to next.

Shared funds of knowledge: the students' community funds of knowledge in developing their learning practices

This section focuses on the relationships that the students forge and the mediations they undertake in their communities to obtain knowledge in constructing their learning practices. From my observations, it was evident that these students' lived experiences necessitated them to make certain adjustments in order to create opportunities for them to learn. Most important to me was the way in which they developed their social networks with other households, and how these households facilitated these social relationships by developing and sharing resources, including their funds of knowledge.

As I asked more questions about the students' customs and networks in the neighbourhood, I realised that they had extensive support networks which included their family, friends and various outreach programmes. From our conversations, I realised early on that their networks were crucially important to them in aspiring to greater heights. They approached it as a dynamic system, which meant that a range of factors and all their interactions contributed to their way of learning, without anything being predetermined, yet also without it being chaotic (Fischer & Bidell 1998).

As I moved around the neighbourhood, I was impressed by what I observed. Until then my knowledge of the area had primarily consisted of the scenes I saw through my car window as I drove there. From my conversations with Ruby, I could sense that her immediate space was of significant practical and social value to her. Amidst difficult circumstances in the neighbourhood, she had to try to carve out opportunities for herself. In this space, Ruby, along with Cherry, Tom, Sally and Musa, attempted to build relationships that served as both a source of motivation and comfort in pursuing their educational objectives. In addition, I concluded from their conversations that the neighbourhood offered them information that helped them realise what it would take to achieve their respective objectives once they finished school. As in many other working-class neighbourhoods, these young people had to adapt to society in order to survive. This caused various sorts of problems between them and their families, as Cherry highlighted by explaining that she is "having a few problems with my parents. We clash because they think differently. One has to adapt to the way of life ... one has to change". This underlines the type of disagreement found within families that occurs between parents and their children.

Nespor (1997) states that physical legacies are shaped by the flow of human activity within and between specific spatial settings. Cherry lives in a modern society, and therefore arranges her life according to society's norms and way of life. Her learning practices, along with those of all her fellow students, are shaped by the dynamic interaction between her thoughts, feelings and social practices in the neighbourhood (Reay 2000, in Fataar 2010). Cherry, Ruby, Sally, Musa and Tom choose to project their learning practices based on the possibilities their community offers. The available options have a positive effect on their lives, achievements and ideals. This, however, also leads them to build relationships outside their homes that are contrary to their families' expectations which results in inner conflict, and which in turn causes the students to develop new ways of seeing themselves in relation to their learning practices. The conflict is further spurred by the different social worlds in which the parents and their children move.

All the students had a sound knowledge of their community. They also displayed a proper knowledge of both local geography (local landmarks, roads) and social networks. I could clearly sense in this rural area a lack of access to the vast array of diverse services available in urban areas. Yet, in addressing this challenge, Tom pointed out that the community "often take the initiative to solve problems ourselves ... or someone [the pastor] with access to our social network [parents, friends, family] intervenes".

Tom told me that many of the people they knew fulfilled various roles in their lives. Moreover, the underlying financial pressure on their parents exacerbated the situation. On more than one occasion, I was also struck by some parents' inability to engage in an academic conversation about their children's schooling. Some of the students' parents had not received much formal schooling, nor were they familiar with the school's educational environment, which in turn affected their children's learning. Yet, despite their circumstances, the students had the benefit of having other people who fulfilled these roles. These people often encouraged them to achieve their full potential and had first-hand knowledge of manipulating systems and networks so that others could benefit. Musa explained how their rural social networks operated. This included how they went about seeking help from friends and neighbours, and gained access to resources, such as by washing a car in exchange for a trip to the mall. When asked to describe the types of social networks in his rural community, Musa said:

> My father has made many friends over the years. Sometimes we call on them to help us with a few things, such as this [pointing to their recently fixed roof]. I mean, the people who helped us know about construction, and when we need help, they come. I think it's a good thing, because I learnt a lot from them.

Musa's words show that these students have access to social networks which help develop the ways in which they solve problems and gain knowledge on what to do in specific situations. At one time, he did however also acknowledge that the neighbourhood failed to equip them with the necessary educational resources to gain access to further studies. According to him, the neighbourhood fails them in two respects: Firstly, the neighbourhood cannot guarantee them access to tertiary study opportunities. Secondly, it cannot provide them with the required skills in order that they can determine what would be required to continue their studies outside the neighbourhood.

Sally also described the type of connections that commonly occurred in her community:

> It's about people. Yes, of course you don't know everyone, but at least you know who lives and works where. You don't have to talk to them because it's your choice. You can't say anything about anyone because it probably is someone else's relative. It's such a small town. It really is very closely knit, and everything and everyone is everyone else's business.

Sally's words illustrate that rural communities develop different forms of social networks.

This section describes the funds of knowledge present in this community at the time of my research. By drawing on these funds the students secured access to valuable community interaction. The knowledge they gained from these encounters would stand them in good stead later on in their search for paid employment. The students were often exposed to practices far removed from the working-class experiences to which they were accustomed in their neighbourhood setting. For this reason they harnessed their strong network of social and material relationships to lend structure to their learning practices. Their social interaction, therefore, was instrumental in positioning their learning practices in their community. Their orientation within the neighbourhood, and the effects of their impoverished setting that they carried with them, had clearly left an indelible mark on their learning practices, which led them to reach out to their peers in establishing their learning practices. This peer interaction is the focus of the following section.

The students' peer-based cultural funds of knowledge in developing their learning practices

This section focuses on how the students collaborated both intentionally and unintentionally within their peer groups to gain access to dominant as well as non-dominant funds of knowledge in their peer group settings. My conversations with the students gave me insight into the various purposes that these different funds of knowledge served. Their descriptions also revealed that they used different forms of knowledge for expressive and instrumental purposes. Instrumentally, they use peer-based funds of knowledge to gain their peers' acceptance as that would guarantee membership of a particular group. Some of them also used dominant peer-based funds of knowledge as a tool to secure academic or job opportunities. Robinson (2000:435) provides the following description of young people's social networks:

> The divisions young people make between places which they find comfortable and those they find threatening or negative, formed on the basis of, and maintained through, the development of socio-spatial networks. The socio-spatial division and network varies depending on personal background and groups with which they strongly agree.

Although the students clearly emphasised the lack of sports and recreational facilities in the area, they did have a vibrant street life and social interaction with their friends in the neighbourhood. When asked what set them apart from other residents in the neighbourhood, it was evident that they experienced their world by establishing cultural boundaries between 'the street', the school and the community. This also tied in with the question of whether they considered their plans for the future to be those of typical young people from their community, to which Tom replied:

> Everyone expects you to behave in a certain way, to hang out with certain people and speak in a certain way. Like, when you're on the streets, you're expected to speak a particular way. It depends on where you are. At school, you're supposed to speak like the people at school. It's how you present yourself. It's like a person with multiple faces.

Here Tom referred to the language strategies deemed appropriate in different social institutions, including those where respect is earned, such as on the streets. Life on the streets as a social space is often characterised by poverty, crime and a cultural 'street code' (Anderson 1999). Tom also gave me various representations of himself. He expressly stated that he would act in a certain way when with his peers on the streets and another way when in the presence of adults. This illustrates how cultural codes operate among youth. Tom's statements are but one example of many instances where the students spoke about the distinction between various backgrounds and explained how they utilised different funds of knowledge in different social settings. Tom and the other students' learning practices are therefore shaped through dynamic interaction with the physical factors around them (Fataar 2010:4). This offers them the formative background against which to shape their learning practices, drawing on their funds of knowledge, amidst the factors imposed on them by their environment.

The students continuously moved around and formed new friendships, which sometimes created new problems. As they moved through the neighbourhood, I realised that they reached out to their friends in their social networks as a tool to select appropriate educational pathways. These networks also offered them the required information on how to follow these pathways, yet without depriving them of the initiative and responsibility of making the final decision themselves. The students regarded their friends as a source of inspiration and information. They often engaged in informal processes by combining various types of social practices and experiences in order to give expression to their learning practices. These students engaged in the social and cultural behaviours of the neighbourhood in different ways, which led to many levels of socialisation and created communication challenges between the youth and their families. In this regard, Ruby remarked:

> Our parents find it difficult to adjust to new things in society, but we are more adaptable. We don't have the same problem. We easily learn to speak the language of the neighbourhood [language among the youth] and don't struggle to make friends.

Like Tom, Ruby too suggested that the youth in the neighbourhood had their own, unique way of communicating. This taught her to be streetwise, which required flexibility and the necessity of having to change her way of thinking in order to cope with the challenges of the neighbourhood that affected her in a negative way. The other students also shaped their learning practices as determined by their everyday activities or, as González (2005:40) puts it, by "what people do and what they say about what they do". The students assigned different meanings to different things, including to some of the elements of traditional neighbourhood values, which helped them develop their emerging learning practices. In order to construct these emerging learning practices, they had to make certain adjustments to align with modern society's culture and values.

To create social and economic opportunities for themselves, the students conceptualised strategies within their peer groups, using all available human resources. Their behaviour was influenced by the way in which they established their social position and addressed problems in their spatial context, as well as by their self-concept as students. Determining their social position, therefore, depends on their social world. Their socialisation practices in their neighbourhood, households and networks centred on the global notion of being well educated and trained. The students' circumstances caused them to think differently about education.

I was told that as the social structures in the neighbourhood changed, so too did their traditional ties, beliefs and social relationships. The students' interviewed revealed that they were also often confronted with a range of questions and options that forced them to choose between their own personal fate and the right way of doing things. This can be ascribed to the way in which modern society presents young people with various choices on all aspects of life, which requires them to make decisions based on more than simply their own personal experiences. Young people, therefore, need to continuously review and adjust their choices and perspectives, in which the media and modern technology play a particularly significant part.

For these students, their peers fulfilled an important role in developing their knowledge. Their peers equipped them with knowledge that adults had not necessarily been able to provide. Their peers also offered them a safe space to express their unique youth culture. Moreover, some of their friends shared their aspirations to achieve success in life which made them realise the importance of learning.

The students' media funds of knowledge in relation to developing their learning practices

I now turn to a focus on the way in which global trends, as driven by information and issues in the media and other global sources, contribute to the construction of the students' learning practices. I support the view that local events are influenced by global trends – the phenomenon commonly referred to as 'globalisation'. According to Comaroff (1996:167), globalisation represents "the material and cultural compression of the world". From observing and interviewing the students, I sensed that they too, like many other young people, favoured a worldview in terms of which global events constitute the most important representative arena for social action and interaction (Mayo 2005). This social action and interaction has a direct impact on them. They experience globalisation on a daily basis through using the internet and cellphones (especially for social networking), as well as through the broader cultural influences affecting their way of life (Kenway & Bullen 2008). Like all other children across the globe, these students are caught up in the global culture. The internet and modern communication technology is part and parcel of their lives. In this regard, Paul Willis (2003) accurately describes young people as "the unconscious foot soldiers in the long front of modernity", stating that:

> ... [while they] respond to global changes in disorganised and chaotic ways, they do so to the best of their abilities and often with relevance to the actual possibilities in their lives as they see, live, and embody them.

Social networks are an important point of reference in relation to which students establish their identity and position themselves in the world. Leander, Phillips and Taylor (2010:362) argue that:

> ... young people who spend time on the Internet are living and learning and moving in and through places and in ways that were not possible only two decades ago.

Participation in social networking sites such as Facebook and Twitter (among others) as well as texting on social media has resulted in new social norms and forms of media literacy. Musa, for example, said: "It's easy to get a message across without having to phrase it perfectly." These students manage their own, unique friendship-driven social and cultural worlds according to their own, internal way of thinking. This is how young people learn to operate in various 'worlds'. It also offers them vital sources of material support in their poorly resourced community. These sources of support help them overcome many challenges and aid their meaningful educational development.

Musa's entire way of life is interlaced with modern technology. He regularly plays computer games and explores the internet as a way of spending time with his friends. The internet also improves his ability to connect with the 'right' type of friends. According to Musa, the improved chat functions on his cellphone have resulted in improved communication with his friends, enabling him to maintain and benefit from local social relationships.

However, Musa's activities are out of keeping with his parents' wishes for how the internet could broaden his global and educational horizons. While his parents had hoped that the internet would develop their children's knowledge of global affairs and literacy, the students prefer to use the internet as a tool to stay in touch with existing friends or to forge ties with new ones. In this regard, Leander *et al* (2010:349) state that "childhood experience of and in space has changed dramatically between generations". Whilst previous generations enjoyed the outdoors, playing in the streets, parks and backyards, the current generation spends more time indoors.

The students all agree that the use of the internet helps them acquire new knowledge and aids their individual learning processes. By using computers (at the local library and school), they develop skills that can be applied in their work environments one day. Their research skills are improved as they grow more confident in utilising the online library to retrieve and access magazine articles for use in school assignments. Their learning is often supported by social media use. The use of social media is generally viewed in a positive light, depending on the type of media employed. Tom articulated this as follows:

> It's sometimes difficult to do my learning activity without the support of media sources ... I learn so many things on my own. Google provides you with so many questions, views and material that you can reflect on and can use as a tool to help you learn.

The students regard active social media use as their way of deepening their reflective abilities. By using social media, they are also forced to review their own personal learning preferences. This, for example, helped Ruby improve her communication skills and learn more independently. She remarked:

> When I do my assignments on the computer, I really enjoy it and find it interesting as the internet offers so many sources and information. I not only use the internet to complete my assignments but also to support what I'm busy learning.

Ruby found the internet the most useful of all media in completing her learning activities. In addition, utilising social media sources during learning activities introduced her to other media forms as well which also benefited her learning activities. Social media use offered Ruby as well as the other students the opportunity to learn from one another.

This section demonstrated how the students in this study engaged in a global culture to construct their learning practices. These practices formed an integral part of their sociability and their youth culture and were central to their learning practice formation.

Conclusion

The aim of this chapter was to shed light on how the students in this study orientated themselves by engaging with funds of knowledge in order to establish their learning practices. I illustrated the diverse and useful funds of knowledge available to these rural secondary school students which they harnessed in order to develop their learning practices and support their learning in general. These funds of knowledge varied, with a few being directly linked to the students' rural background. Their ability to develop strategic relationships and networks played a major part in the construction of their learning practices. A range of strategies were employed to access their funds of knowledge. The students were forced to make certain adjustments in order to develop their learning practices which led each of them to identify a unique set of knowledge funds to apply in their learning. In the process the students acquired a wide variety of interests and skills. By engaging with their funds of knowledge they were able to effectively address their learning challenges.

My key analytical conclusion in the study on which this chapter is based is that these students were able to turn to, and use, certain funds of knowledge in a logical and reasoned manner in order to construct their learning practices. They displayed the ability to mobilise and harness all the essential sources for developing their learning practices in their social settings. Their learning practices also often clashed with their need to fit in with the activities of their families, the community and their peers.

In this chapter, I have presented the key argument that working-class rural students use their funds of knowledge as a vehicle to develop their learning practices. Instead of openly protesting against what is happening in their neighbourhood, they take part in their neighbourhood culture. My interviews and observations have shown that students learn by means of various sources of knowledge, networks and interaction with people and processes, thereby finding their own, unique way of constructing their learning practices. By making small adjustments to their way of thinking and acting, the students systematically build their emerging learning practices. This, however, does not constitute a total transformation of behaviour and thought – the adjustments are minor in the sense that the students are still constrained by their circumstances. These students remain caught up in their impoverished existence; yet they are determined to stay the course in terms of their schooling. My discussion and analysis has also revealed how working-class students accept responsibility for, and become involved in, their educational practices – an aspect not often explored in research on this topic.

References

Anderson E. 1999. *Code of the street: Decency, violence, and the moral life of the inner city*. New York: WW Norton.

Bourdieu P. 2006. "The forms of capital". In: H Lauder, P Brown, JA Dillabough & AH Halsey (eds). *Education, Globalisation and Social Change*. Oxford: Oxford University Press.

Clark J. 2008. "Research Methods". Postgraduate dissertation (unpublished). University of the Western Cape.

Comaroff JL. 1996. "Ethnicity, nationalism, and the politics of difference in an age of revolution". In: EN Wilmsen & P McAllister (eds). 1996. *The Politics of Difference: Ethnic Premises in a World of Power*. Chicago: University of Chicago Press.

Fataar A. 2010. Youthful becoming and rural-urban mobility: the case of Fuzile Ali at a Muslim community school in Cape Town. *Southern African Review of Education*, 15(2):105–117.

Fataar A. 2015. *Engaging schooling subjectivities across post-apartheid urban spaces*. Stellenbosch: AFRICAN SUN MeDIA. https://doi.org/10.18820/9781920689834

Fataar A & Du Plooy L. 2012. Spatialised assemblages and suppressions: The learning 'positioning' of Grade 6 students in a township school. *Journal of Education*, 55:7–23.

Fillies H. 2015. "Die konstruering van hoërskool leerders se leerpraktyke binne 'n werkersklaswoonbuurt" [The construction of high school learners' learning practices in a working class neighbourhood] (unpublished dissertation). Stellenbosch University.

Fischer KW & Bidell TR. 1998. "Dynamic development of psychological structures in action and thought". In: W Damon & RM Lerner (eds). *Handbook of child psychology: theoretical models of human development* (5th Edition, Volume 1). NY: Wiley & Sons. 467–562.

González N. 2005. "Beyond culture: The hybridity of funds of knowledge". In: N González, LC Moll & C Amanti (eds). 2005. *Funds of Knowledge: Theorizing Practices in Households, Communities, and Classrooms*. Mahwah, NJ: Lawrence Erlbaum Associates. 29–47.

González N, Moll LC & Amanti C (eds). 2005. *Funds of Knowledge: Theorizing Practices in Households, Communities and Classrooms*. Mahwah, NJ: Lawrence Erlbaum Associates.

Kenway J & Bullen E. 2008. "The global corporate curriculum and the young cyberflaneur as Global Citizen". In: N Dolby & F Rizvi (eds). *Youth Moves – Identities and education in global perspectives*. New York: Routledge.

Leander K, Phillips N & Taylor K. 2010. The changing social spaces of learning: Mapping new identities. *Review of Research in Education*, 34:329–394. https://doi.org/10.3102/0091732X09358129

Mayo M. 2005. *Global citizens: Social movements and the challenge of globalisation*. London: Zed Books.

Moll LC 1992. Bilingual classrooms and community analysis: Some recent trends. *Educational Researcher*, 21(2):20–24. https://doi.org/10.3102/0013189X021002020

Moll L, Amanti C, Neff D & González N. 1992. Funds of knowledge for teaching: Using a qualitative approach to developing strategic connections between homes and classrooms. *Theory into Practice*, 31(2):132–141. https://doi.org/10.1080/00405849209543534

Nespor J. 1997. *Tangled up in school: Politics, space, bodies and signs in the educational process*. London: Laurence Erlbaum.

Neuman WL. 2011. *Social research methods: Qualitative and quantitative methods*. 7th Edition. Boston: Allyn & Bacon.

Phillips L. 1999. *Australian storytelling: The role of storytelling in early literacy development*. http://www.australianstorytelling.org [Accessed 27 March 2013].

Robinson C. 2000. Creating space, creating self: Street frequenting youth in the city and suburbs. *Journal of Youth Studies*, 3(4):429–443. https://doi.org/10.1080/713684388

Willis P. 2003. Foot soldiers of modernity: The dialectics of cultural consumption and the 21st-century school. *Harvard Educational Review*, 73(3):390–415. https://doi.org/10.17763/haer.73.3.0w5086336u305184

Chapter 4

"Playing the game": High school students' mediation of their educational subjectivities across dissonant fields

Nazli Domingo-Salie

Introduction

This chapter draws on my research in rural and urban working-class environments in the Western Cape Province of South Africa, and a Focus School located in a middle-class area in Cape Town. The chapter focuses on the navigational practices of four historically disadvantaged students who accomplished their education 'on the move' between their working-class domestic environment and the dissonant terrain of the Focus School situated in a middle-class suburb. The discussion presented focuses on how selected black and coloured students from rural and urban working-class areas in the Western Cape adapted, shifted and established their educational subjectivities while attending a Focus School over a period of three years. This chapter employs the lens of 'trans-locating habitus' to describe the practices that the four students employed in order to navigate the initially dissonant terrain of the Focus School and presents an argument for how the four students, via their navigational practices between their domestic environment and the Focus School, established a trans-local habitus. The aim of this chapter is to open up a window into how historically disadvantaged students establish their educational subjectivities across different social spaces. I use the stories of the four students to illustrate how young people 'trans-locate' between working-class domestic environments and institutions in middle-class settings.

It was during my visits (as an education specialist) to schools that had performed well in the Western Cape Education Department (WCED) standardised systemic tests that I came across a Focus School in a middle-class area that serviced historically disadvantaged students. Being a person who had experienced educational disadvantage myself, my interest was sparked regarding the practices of these students who came from working-class environments, and who had produced excellent results by attending the Focus School.

I considered that a trans-local habitus is a necessary requirement for individuals who are born and raised in disadvantaged conditions, but who go on to figure out how to succeed in different, often culturally alienating terrains such as the Focus School that was situated in a middle-class locale. This chapter makes the argument that it is the development of a trans-local habitus that enables these students, in effect, to have a shot at successfully engaging in the educational 'game of schooling'.

I offer the notion of 'trans-local habitus' as an analytical construct by drawing on a number of different aspects. Practices of persons who move between different locales without losing sight of the importance of the localities in which they are situated, are described by Oakes and Schein (2006) as *trans-localism*. Similarly, I draw on the explanation Fataar (2015) offers when he uses *trans-location* to refer to the movement of individuals across different spaces and Man and Cohen's (2015) concept of *trans-nationalism*, to discuss the movement of individuals across different locales. This chapter primarily focuses on Levitt's (2001) description of *trans-local habitus* as one that involves practices and relations across different social spaces, and the ability to live and feel at home in more than one space.

Of the four students I chose via snowball sampling, Luke, Phumla and TK were from rural towns, while Mona was from the city. All four students attended schools in their working-class areas up to Grade 9, and then attended the Focus School from Grade 10 to Grade 12. Drawing on qualitative strategies in order to gain an understanding of the trans-locating practices of the four students, three in-depth, semi-structured one-hour interviews were conducted with each interviewee at venues that were conveniently located. Qualitative research methodology was considered the most suitable to gain insight into how the four students mediated their trans-local habitus in an educational institution such as a Focus School to achieve academic success.

Post-1994, during the educational reform of the new government, Focus Schools were established by the WCED as an attempt to increase the number of students matriculating in Mathematics and Science and Technology. Students attending schools in working-class environments post-1994 were still struggling to achieve educational success due to overcrowding, lack of resources and inadequately qualified teachers, to name but a few of the challenges that schools in black and coloured areas experienced due to the legacy of the apartheid era. The Focus School, which was a boarding school facility established in 2004, aimed to support historically disadvantaged students who showed potential in Mathematics and Science and Technology.

Students attending the Focus School were required to become weekly boarders at the school. For many of these students there was a significant disjuncture between their domestic environment and the new locale of the Focus School. This required that they find ways to embody the requirements of the Focus School in order to become successful students. This chapter aims to show how the four students navigated across various spatial terrains in order to develop successful educational subjectivities at the Focus School, what I refer to as the mediation of a trans-local habitus.

'Trans-location' as a term refers to the movement of individuals across different spaces (Fataar 2015). For the students in this study, I apply the term trans-local habitus to understand the students' mobility between their domestic environment and the Focus School and the adaptations they made across these spaces to become successful students. Trans-location provides a lens for understanding how students establish their educational subjectivity on the move. Thus, trans-local habitus refers to the construction of an adapted habitus which, through the students' mobility, enabled them to become conceptually mobile adaptive readers of space, and go on to figure out how to succeed in their education in a hitherto 'alien' territory.

This study draws on Bourdieu's concepts of habitus and field to discuss how the students shifted and adapted their habitus to the requirements of the Focus School. Bourdieu's concepts of habitus and field, augmented by Urry's theorisation of mobility, provide a theoretical lens that allows me to analyse how the four students established successful educational subjectivities on the move. Bourdieu defines one's habitus as "an open system of dispositions that is constantly subjected to experiences, and therefore constantly affected by them in a way that either reinforces or modifies its structures" (Bourdieu & Wacquant 1992:133). According to Bourdieu, the dispositions associated with habitus predispose individuals to choose behaviour which appears to them to achieve the desired outcome given their previous experiences, the resources available to them, and the prevailing state of the field. In this way habitus, as a system of transposable dispositions, guides an individual's actions in a social space (Bourdieu 1977:82–83). Calhoun describes the process that an individual embarks on to cope with changes in the field, as a practical reaction to a situation based on experience, combined with an embodied sensibility that leads to a structured improvisation of the habitus (2000:712, in Hillier & Rooksby 2005:22). Bourdieu notes that, as habitus is constituted in practice and is "always orientated to practical functions", it is constantly subjected to a range of different experiences which will either reinforce or modify the dispositions of the habitus (1980:52). Thus, Bourdieu accepts that one's habitus can be modified; habitus "is durable but not eternal" (Bourdieu & Wacquant 1992:133).

The four students in this study were required to shift and adapt their subjectivities to the new school field environment in order to achieve their future educational goals. Bourdieu states that an individual's practical relation to the future, which defines one's present behaviour, consists of the relationship between habitus and the opportunities offered to them, and is therefore "constructed in the course of a particular relationship to a particular universe of probabilities" (1980:64). In this way the four students' "sense of the probable future" was constituted through their relationship "with a world structured according to the categories of the possible … and the impossible" (Bourdieu 1980:64). The changes that the four students made, therefore, by shifting and adapting their educational subjectivities to match the requirements of the Focus School field, can be described as a "selective perception of a situation which generates a response according to the practical potential of satisfying the actor/s' desire/s" (Hillier & Rooksby 2005:23–24).

Bourdieu terms the socially structured space, in which activities occur, a field. A field is a "relational configuration endowed with a specific gravity which it imposes on all the objects and agents which enter in it" (Bourdieu & Wacquant 1992:17). A field, as a social space, is also a space of conflict and competition where individuals struggle to achieve their aims. Bourdieu employs the analogy of a 'game' to describe how individuals work to improve their positions in a social field. To be successful in a game requires not just understanding and following the rules of the game, but involves players having a sense of the game:

> It requires constant awareness of and responsiveness to the play of all actors involved. It requires assessment of one's own team-mates/s' resources, strengths and weaknesses and also those of the opponent/s. It requires improvisation and flexibility and above all it requires use of anticipation as to what one's team-mate/s and one's opponent/s will do. Behaviours cannot be reduced simply to theoretical rules.   (Hillier & Rooksby 2005:23)

It is in learning to play by the 'rules of the game' (written and unwritten) that the four students within the social space of the Focus School environment, learned how to modify their behaviour in order to work effectively within the existing practices of the new field. In other words, they learned what was possible (or not) within the rules and regularities of the Focus School field. In this manner, when the four students were faced with new field conditions, they began to figure out what they could do based on their own limits and abilities and, in this way, chose their adapted course of action given the new field circumstances.

For the four students discussed in this chapter, their initial move to the social field of the Focus School was fraught with unease and anxiety. The Focus School was initially alienating and discordant to their working-class home environments. The written and unwritten 'rules of the game' of the new school were significantly different to those of their previous school. Being weekly boarders added a further dimension to the students' changed lives, as none of the four students had ever lived away from their home environments before.

In order to become adept within the new field environment of the Focus School the four students had to shift and adapt their educational subjectivities to 'fit' the requirements of their new school field. This required them to develop social competency and fluid and adaptable subjectivities to play by the 'rules' of the new 'game'. Webb, Schirato and Danaher (2002:38) note that the habitus is constituted "in moments of practice" when an individual's set of dispositions meets a particular problem or context with which it is not familiar. Thus, for the four students, the challenges of the new school context required them to find ways to shift and adapt their dispositions in order to learn to 'play the game' in the new field. It is this that Bourdieu refers to as acquiring a 'feel for the game', i.e. developing a habitus-field match, and which enables an individual to become a successful player in a new field environment.

The four students in this study are considered mobile students, in that they moved weekly from their domestic environment to the Focus School field. Thus, Bourdieu's analogy of 'playing the game', combined with Urry's theory of mobility, provided a lens that allowed me to understand and explain how the four students adapted their subjectivities to the rules and regularities of the different field contexts 'on the move'.

The conceptualisation of subjectivity is taken from Hall (2004) who describes one's subjectivity as something that is always produced or created from the ingredients of one's past, and is always in the process of transformation. Elliot and Urry (2010), in their discussion on the development of mobile lives, describe a number of subjective transformations that individuals make and which create what they describe as a 'field of mobilities'. Relevant to this study is the "centrality of mobilities in people's social and emotional lives" (Elliot & Urry 2010:59). They describe how mobilities, as a distinct field, is characterised by "struggles, tastes and habituses ... a site of multiple intersecting contestations" (Elliot & Urry 2010:59). They go on to argue that it is through the embodiment of an individual's experiences 'on the move', as a form of network and social capital, that one is able to engender and sustain social relations with those we encounter within our social fields. For the four students the 'field of mobility', therefore, applies to the manner in which they were able to successfully move between the two distinct fields, drawing on the network and social capital in both fields, to shift and adapt their educational subjectivities to the requirements of each field environment.

Focus Schools were established in 2004 by the Western Cape Education Department (WCED) as an attempt to increase the numbers of the students matriculating in

Maths and Science and Technology. Historically disadvantaged students who showed education ability and tenacity were recruited from schools in the Western Cape to attend this school. It is located in a middle-class area, was well-resourced and had teachers who were experts in their fields. The students stayed in the school hostel during the week and went home on the weekends.

Each of the students experienced life within the space of their working-class domestic environment differently. Mona, from an urban area, received minimal educational support from her family, but her family had strong religious and traditional affiliations. Despite her domestic environment being rather dysfunctional, she attended a former Model C primary school before attending a working-class high school, prior to attending the Focus School. Luke's life in a rural town was afflicted with tensions in the home. The loss of his father, however, resulted in a positive attitude and his positioning and identity as a student. The responsibilities he had as a child provided him with the ability and maturity to adjust to diverse situations. Phumla's stable home life and movement between rural and urban schools suggests a complicated evolution of her subjective awareness as a student. Moving from one spatial terrain to the other served to develop her survival and coping mechanisms allowing her to exploit each space to her benefit. Similarly, TK's stable home life in a rural town and the relationships that he had in his upbringing, served as key elements in shaping his identity as a student. This accorded him the opportunity to have the ability to adapt and become active in different environments. I suggest, therefore, that domestic and institutional factors were key in supporting the students' ability to adapt from their domestic environment to the Focus School.

Bourdieu's analogy of playing the game, allows me to describe how the students adapted their practices to apply the 'rules and regularities' of the Focus School field to become competent players of the game. First, on arrival at the Focus School, the students were confronted with 'new rules' of the game, which they needed to learn and apply in order to be successful in the new school field environment. Mona had this to say of her initial alienation:

> We were provided with a list of assignments for the term with due dates ...
> and we were actually expected to hand them in on the due dates. I had never
> done homework before.

Students were required to learn how to play by the 'rules' in the new school field in order to become successful. TK reported that he had to grow up quickly and organise and plan his time better. This socialisation called for the students to learn the new social rules at the Focus School in order to fit in and play the game successfully.

In order to attain social competencies, the students were compelled to align their habitus to the values and imperatives of the Focus School. Bourdieu describes this as 'playing the game'. Phumla commented on the fact that she started to mature faster when she got to the Focus School. She said: "I saw that things were different here. I had to work harder. I had to be responsible." Luke formed working groups that sat together in the passage at night after lights out. The students realised that the way they comported themselves at the Focus School needed to be different to the way they had behaved at their previous schools.

Continuing with Bourdieu's metaphor, of 'playing the game', the students now began to embody the rules of the game. This embodiment involved the students shifting and adapting their habitus to align to the rules and regulations of the new school field. Mona had this to say:

> I had a much better understanding of the work. It made me want to engage more in learning. I approached the teachers who were always willing to assist us, and I utilised resources even after school hours.

Over time the students came to invest themselves in the new field environment and no longer wanted to return home over the weekends.

'Playing the game' successfully in the new school environment required the students to shift and adapt their educational subjectivities, develop social competency and a fluid and adaptable habitus in order to meet the requirements of the Focus School. In other words, a successful *trans-local habitus* is one that allows the individual, via their navigation across different fields, to successfully adapt their dispositions (habitus) to the rules and regularities of the new field context.

Trans-local habitus at the Focus School

This section now goes on to focus on the complex ways in which the four historically disadvantaged students mediated their educational subjectivities at the Focus School. One of the students was selected by his former high school to attend the school, one student's parents organised her application, while two of the students themselves decided to apply to attend the Focus School. The respondents in my study were termed 'designer' students by the principal of the Focus School. The reason given by all four students for attending the school was their aspiration to acquire successful educational subjectivities.

As a broad definition, the concept of student educational subjectivity that I use in this chapter is based on an understanding of the ways in which individuals encounter the worlds of their schooling, and how their subjectivities are established in light of their educational and social practices (Fataar 2009). Within the 'game' (Bourdieu 1990), what determines the extent to which an agent is able to master the regularities (as opposed to the rules) of a particular field, is their habitus. According to Bourdieu and Wacquant (1992:63), "Habitus as a feel for the game is the social game embodied and turned into a second nature. Nothing is simultaneously freer and more constrained than the action of the good player."

A student whose habitus does not match the school's values, attitudes and dispositions will more than likely find the school to be "a very alien and hostile environment" (Webb *et al* 2002:114). It was this initial 'mismatch' experienced by the students, which can be described as a form of alienation between their domestic habitus and the new field environment, i.e. the Focus School, which required the students to shift and change their practices in order to establish a successful educational subjectivity.

Subjectivity can be described as what the students become or how they develop their sense of self as they interact with the dynamics present in a specific context. For Woodward (1997:39), subjectivity relates to the unconscious and conscious emotions and thoughts in a social context. She claims that individuals experience their subjectivities in a social context where language and culture gives meaning to their experiences of themselves and where they adopt identities. The things that make them who they are exist within a cultural context, i.e. the context in which they live, where they have come from, and where they are headed.

In order for the four students to successfully shift their educational subjectivities to align with the requirements of the new school field, it was necessary for them to interact both physically and conceptually with the different 'spaces' at the Focus School. The four respondents' prior educational subjectivities were differently framed by their embodied experiences within domestic environments which had shaped their educational identities. Of these experiences TK had this to say:

> I have lived in Wolmarans all my life. My parents who are hardworking, are good role models for me. They sent me to what they thought were the best schools for me in the coloured area of Wolmarans. My parents and grandmother also instilled good education values in me. They always had time to take me and my sister on camping trips during the December holidays.

Similarly, Phumla, who came from a stable home, expressed that:

> I come from a diverse family. My mom and dad were ambitious. That is where I get it from. In order to improve our lives, we moved across various towns in the Western Province. We always owned our homes. They taught me to be spiritual, and I remember us spending many happy times together as a family.

Despite not having homes as stable as Phumla and TK, Luke and Mona experienced a measure of functionality within their homes created by extended family members. Of this, Luke had to say:

> My mom who divorced my dad before I could remember, always worked hard to provide for us which left my grandmother (Mom's mother) to take care of us when we were young. After the death of my father when I was eight years old, his mother (my other granny), made sure that my brother and I experienced family outings such as picnics ... Between my grandparents, I experienced great support and lovely traditions over Christmas and Easter.

Mona stated that:

> I don't know how my grandparents managed to take care of me and my three siblings, in addition to their own three children who still lived in the house ... hey? We were always fed and they made sure that we went to, what they thought, were good schools. They taught us to be spiritual and attend church, and that family took care of one another. I learnt from them that I must work hard if I want something out of life.

On arrival at the Focus School the students found themselves in a new field environment. Bourdieu describes a field as a "structured social space" that contains "people with constant and permanent relationships that operate within this space by either transforming or preserving the space by defining their position within the space" (1998:40–41). Thus, the four students found themselves within new social structures which required that they shifted and changed their individualised actions in order to begin to rearticulate and adapt their individual educational subjectivities.

The students were from a variety of different rural and urban schools who moved from their domestic environments to attend the Focus School. Elliot and Urry (2010) state that in order to become mobile individuals draw on a form of 'network capital', and it is through this 'network capital' that they are able to create a mobile field which enables them to access new experiences. They call this a 'field of mobility' (Elliot & Urry 2010). The mobility for these students involved travelling between 12 to 109 kilometres from their homes to the Focus School as well as living in a different environment from that of their normal homes.

Despite the initial excitement, my respondents found themselves questioning whether they had made the right decision to attend the Focus School. Attendance at the Focus School was not as easy as they thought it would be. For some, they had left close and supportive family members behind, and they missed their siblings. Luke notes that: "... although I was excited to leave home, I was very close to my brother and sister and it was not easy to leave them behind." Phumla was worried about leaving her family and disclosed that: "We are a very close family and as the eldest child, I usually help my siblings with their homework. I worried that I was not there for them." Mona and TK described the practical aspects of moving away from home that worried them thus:

> I had very long hair that I wore in plaits [braids]. Besides missing my sister with whom I shared a room all my life, I worried how I was going to manage my hair. (Mona)

TK put it this way:

> I had never lived away from home. My parents were always there to guide me. I worried who was going to give me guidance at the Focus School.

Arriving at a school environment, which was significantly different to their previous school, created an element of unease and trepidation. All four students were of the opinion that only the brightest students from historically disadvantaged schools were chosen to attend the Focus School. They realised that the academic standards of the Focus School would be significantly higher than their previous schools, and they feared that they would not be able to meet the expectations of the school. It was the first time these students were navigating a school field that was different to the schools they had attended in their domestic environment, coupled with the additional challenge of attending a boarding school. They had varied levels of anxiety as expressed below:

> I was a bit nervous. Suddenly, I longed to be back at my former high school. I was involved with music at the school, and that is what I was sorry about leaving behind. (Mona)

When probed why she felt that way, Mona responded:

> I felt that I did not come from the best of schools. I was anxious. I do not regard myself as a confident person. I kept to myself. They did say these were the brightest students. I thought that everyone is brighter than me.

Phumla, whose parents had made the decision for her to attend the school, expressed that: "I heard that this was a Maths and Science school. I was afraid that I would not keep up with the other students and that I would fail." Doubting his self-discipline in the absence of his parents, TK also expressed his anxiety:

> It was a challenge to be away from home as a 15-year-old. There was no more guidance from my parents. The first week was really hard. I missed home so much, I wanted to withdraw from the Focus School and return to my old school.

Luke feared that if he did not work hard enough, he would have to return to his former working-class high school. He commented that he:

> ... feared that I would have to return to Pula if I did not make it here. The embarrassment of having to return to Pula because I thought I was smart. I could just foresee all the nasty crap people would say.

Here the students are expressing their concern that their educational subjectivities are not congruent with the educational expectations of the Focus School. Bourdieu's analogy of a game (Bourdieu & Wacquant 1992:63) assists us to understand the role that habitus and field play in the logic of practice. The students at the Focus School were confronted with new 'rules of the game' which they needed to learn and apply in order to be successful in the new school field environment. Luke describes an example of their initial alienation at the Focus School and the manner in which they had to shift and adapt their educational subjectivities to the new school regularities: "School started on time, and the teachers were in the classroom at the start of the lesson." Confronted by the new rules of the game in the new field environment of the Focus School, the students needed to understand the structures and rules implicit in the field and find ways in which they could re-position their educational subjectivities in order to become successful in the new educational field.

The students experienced their educational socialisation differently between their domestic environment and the Focus School. This required that they adapt their subjectivities in order to play by the new rules of the game as required by the school field context. By attending the Focus School, the students had to change their behaviour in order to 'fit in' at the new school as the Focus School's social and educational expectations were, according to all four students, very different to their home environments and that of their former schools.

Educational socialisation at the Focus School

Socialisation can be defined as the process by which the students at the Focus School learned the ways of behaving, or, as Bourdieu states, learned to 'play the game', in order to function successfully within it. It was an understanding of, and adapting to new ways of socialisation that provided a conduit that enabled the four students to traverse the expectations of the Focus School. This process of socialisation required the students to learn new social 'rules' in order to 'fit in' and play the game successfully. In other words, the students learnt to be concerned with what was expected and appropriate behaviour in the new school field as a general guide to their conduct. They developed a sense of propriety, which governed their behaviour and which, in turn, guided them in dealing with the new situations they encountered for the first time at the Focus School.

Examples of social differences that the students encountered were found in the organisational structures of the school as well as the expectations of the teachers. The students noticed that the standards of the school were higher than their previous schools and, whereas before they had been able to easily achieve good marks, they now had to work much harder than before. The students also observed that the school had more resources to support their learning and that the teachers were specialists in the subjects they taught. TK stated that at his former school it often took a week or two to finalise timetables and to organise stationery before teaching commenced. In contrast, TK noted:

> The Focus School, was ready on the first day as we arrived. We were given our timetable, stationery and text books before the classes started. The classes started immediately after we completed the registration process.

TK recalled the difference he felt in the classroom: "The students who surrounded me were A-Grade, motivated students. The workload was more and the pace was faster." When asked whether TK was prepared for the Focus School, he responded: "Yes. I feel that I was mature. But I still doubted that I would cope with the Maths and Physics."

Luke was initially quite confident that he would cope with Mathematics at the Focus School, since he had consistently scored high marks at his former school. He was therefore shocked at his results after the first baseline Mathematics test. He relates the following:

> I failed my first Maths test. I was horrified. We had a very good teacher, and we got a test out of ten. I remember. It was just to place the class and see where you are at, and for him to see where you are at. I got two out of ten! God ... I almost killed myself! I love Maths, and had breezed through it before.

The four students all noted that they initially feared that they would be behind with their work. This fear made them realise that they needed to find ways to adapt to the requirements of the new school field if they were to achieve their aspirations. Mona pointed out that she too had noticed that the dynamics of the school were very different to those of her previous high school. It appeared as if every student was there to learn. She noted: "All the students were paying attention to the teachers during class!"

Establishing one's subjectivity is not something that occurs automatically (Elkin & Handel 1989). In keeping with Bourdieu's analogy of a game (Bourdieu & Wacquant 1992:63) the students came to realise that they needed to find out the 'rules', both the implicit and explicit social rules, and begin to 'play' by the 'rules of the game' at the Focus School. In other words, in order for the students to be socialised into the field of the Focus School, they had to learn and develop a 'sense of propriety' that enabled them to conform to what was socially acceptable behaviour in the new field environment. This resulted in the students having to make significant adjustments by the end of the first week of the first term due to the workload and structure at the Focus School. TK reported that he felt that he had to grow up quickly and organise and plan his time better. He also noted that, as a way of learning how to socialise in the new school field or, as Bourdieu describes it, to 'learn the rules of the game', that "support from my fellow classmates also helped".

In my interviews with the students, they reflected that living in the school hostel allowed them more time for their education as they were relieved of the chores and responsibilities that they had had at home. They realised that in order to meet the requirements of the educational expectations of the school they needed to significantly adapt their educational subjectivities if they were to achieve their aspirations. Luke feared that if he did not work hard enough, he would have to return to his former working-class high school.

Living in close proximity with the other students afforded the four students the opportunity to build support groups as a form of educational socialisation. Luke describes how he:

> ... set up a group of students from Pula as a support group. I had to make drastic changes. I was self-conscious of not being on the same level of the other students. I made use of the school's set times for study, and the venues which were made available.

Phumla's ambition was to become a doctor, and it was this that drove her to embrace the culture and high expectations of the school. She noted: "We were placed in classes according to our academic ability. I would work hard to make sure that I would not be placed in the lower classes."

The analogy of 'playing the game', shows how the students came to realise that they needed to employ different strategies to maintain or improve their position in the new school field environment. Furthermore, they developed social competencies and practices that enabled them to begin to shift and adapt their educational subjectivities successfully at the Focus School.

Attaining social competency

The students developed social competencies at the Focus School that allowed them to construct successful school lives. In other words, they developed practices that helped them to shift their educational subjectivities to incorporate dispositions that supported their successful integration into the Focus School. These practices involved finding ways to develop social competency by coming to understand and to follow the rules and regulations of the new school field. For the four students this involved aligning their habitus to the values and imperatives of the Focus School. Bourdieu notes that successful relations in a field, such as the field of education, are closely linked to how an individual acquires an appropriate disposition, which aligns their habitus with the field structure. Bourdieu reminds us, though, that within a social field, unlike a game, these rules are often not explicit, and what determines the extent to which an individual is able to master the regularities of a particular field is their ability to learn the tempo, rhythms and unwritten rules of the game. Thus, to understand and come to master a particular practice in order to 'play the game' well, an individual must gain a feel for the practical logic of the game, i.e. the regularities of the game. Bourdieu states that it is through one's habitus that mastery of this practical logic takes place (Bourdieu 1990:63). Consequently, changing or adapting one's habitus requires one to find new ways in which to respond to cultural rules and contexts of the new field.

On arrival at the school, the students quickly came to realise that in order for them to become successful in the new school field they needed to shift and adapt the way they engaged with and managed their learning. In other words, they had to find ways to gain certain social competencies that would enable them to navigate their schooling successfully. The Focus School made certain rules and expectations clear. For example, they had to be punctual, achieve certain marks in their tests to stay at the school, and they had to take part in extra-curricular activities. However, as with most 'fields', the Focus School field operated on a set of unwritten rules which implicitly governed the successful integration of the students into the new school field environment. For the students, these unwritten rules of the game, the underlying practices within the Focus School, were the competencies that they endeavoured to embody in order to be successful in the new school field environment. Regarding this Phumla expressed that:

> I was so excited. If I did what the school expected of me, then I could reach my dreams of becoming a doctor! Being at the Focus School, made me want to make a success of my life.

The students realised that the way in which they comported themselves at the Focus School needed to be different to the way that they had behaved in their previous schools. They recognised that they needed to adapt their educational dispositions developed in their previous school environment to meet the requirements of the Focus School. In other words, their habitus, as a 'socialised subjectivity', and the 'social embodiment' emanating from their domestic and previous school environments, needed to shift and change to adapt to the new field requirements. Reay notes that, "when habitus encounters a field with which it is not familiar, the resulting dis-junctures can generate change and transformation" (2004:436). Therefore, in order to work towards developing successful educational subjectivities and social competencies that aligned with the Focus School requirements, the four students needed to adapt their habitus to the requirements of the new school field.

The students realised that particular strategies, such as having effective time management, working collaboratively, utilising resources available to them, and learning to interact with their teachers regarding aspects of their school work, would assist them to become successful at their new school. Luke describes how utilising these strategies enabled him to begin to develop social competency:

> I started to focus better by adopting ideas from the school. I put in the extra effort. It was a strain as we would study in our dorms [dormitories] at night. But there were eight people there and lights were put off at ten o'clock. I used to sit in the hallways at night and do extra Maths. Sometimes other students would join me.

One of the ways in which the school was structured was that the boys and girls had separate hostels. The four students explained that within the hostels the students formed study groups according to the two main languages used at the school, English and Afrikaans. These study groups became an important mechanism by which the students developed social competencies which enabled them to cope with the pressures of the Focus School. Mona describes how she spent most of her leisure time with the English-speaking female students, and that it was this peer group which was instrumental in supporting her aspirations. She noted that:

> What I had in common with the other students was that we were all focused. The smarter students hung out together. I was always in the top ten. We [the students] used to all be up late at night, and we would help each other study.

TK and Luke had peers from their former high schools that attended the Focus School with them. Together they formed a group to support their learning. Their accounts regarding this issue are given below:

> My brother arrived at the Focus School a year after me, and together with two of my friends from my former high school, we formed a group that supported one another in our school work.   (Luke)

> It really helped to work in groups. When you sit with others who understand the work better than you do it helps you.   (TK)

Another strategy that enabled the four students to become competent and successful was their ability to identify and use the resources available at the school. Phumla described the situation thus:

> There was excellent support from the teachers at the Focus School. They [the teachers] helped me with Maths and Biology. I attended the extra classes that they provided. I had fostered good relationships with my teachers.

As the transcripts above indicate, the students developed strategies that allowed them to respond to the cultural rules and contexts which confronted them at the Focus School. These strategies included finding ways to shift their dispositions to include adapted social competencies that they learned through their interactions at the school site. These competencies enabled them to construct the practices that allowed them to become good 'players of the game' at the Focus School. Bourdieu and Wacquant (1992:23) state that a good player is one:

> ... who is so to speak, the game incarnate, does at every moment what the game requires. That presupposes a permanent capacity for invention, indispensable if one is to be able to adapt to indefinitely varied and never completely identical situation.

Thus, it was the students' 'capacity for invention' that enabled them to learn the new regularities of the Focus School and acquire the social competencies necessary for developing a trans-local habitus that would enable them to successfully integrate into the new field. The establishment of their trans-local habitus was as a result of the students' fluid and adaptable educational subjectivities in relation to their navigation at the Focus School.

Fluid and adaptable subjectivities at the Focus School

The four students navigated the social spaces of the new school environment in order to adopt fluid and adaptable subjectivities which would enable them to become successful at the Focus School. I previously described how the students meditated their subjectivities via their socialisation practices and the development of social competencies at the Focus School. These practices worked together to develop the students' fluid and adaptable subjectivities that enabled them to cultivate a trans-local habitus.

Continuing with Bourdieu's metaphor of 'playing a game', this section describes how the students began to embody the rules of the game in the new school field in order to become successful 'players' at the Focus School. This embodiment involved the students shifting and adapting their habitus to align to the rules and regulations of the new school field. Bourdieu notes that habitus and field are relational in that they operate only in relation to one another, and a field is seen, "as a space of play which exists as such only to the extent that players enter into it who believe in and actively pursue the prizes it offers … [c]onversely, the theory of habitus is incomplete without a notion of structure that makes room for the organised improvisation of agents" (Bourdieu & Wacquant 1992:19). As such, the four students, through their investment in the structures of the new school field, over time adopted fluid and adaptable subjectivities that enabled them to become successful students.

To embody the rules and regulations of the Focus School the students engaged in a range of behaviours. These behaviours included a strategic reading of the Focus School's cultural functioning and expectations, many of which differed significantly from their previous school. During my interviews, the students identified a variety of activities and resources that supported their successful transitioning into the new school environment. These included: living on the school premises, longer school hours, after-hours support, sporting and cultural activities, access to science laboratories and library facilities, availability of text books and technology, as well as well-qualified teachers. The four students stated that not only did these activities and resources support their learning, they also created an educational climate that was significantly different to their previous schools. The students describe the Focus School as having a culture of teaching and learning that included high academic expectations combined with an investment in the aspirations of the students to study in tertiary institutions when they left the school. In this regard Mona notes that:

> I had a much better understanding of the work. It made me want to engage more in learning. There was a well-resourced Science lab. Even the teachers, as resources outside school hours … they were amazing. They [the teachers] were always approachable … and always willing to help.

In discussing how the culture of teaching and learning provided opportunities that they had not had before, Mona proudly mentioned that: "I won the Lego competition that was hosted at the MTN Science Centre, I would not have had that opportunity at my old school." Similarly, the students were provided with opportunities to develop leadership skills. In this regard, Phumla states that:

> I knew that I had leadership qualities. I was chosen to be a member of the student council called the Representative Student Council (RCL). This was new to me.

Not only did the school provide them with new opportunities, it also assisted them to raise the necessary funds to take up the opportunities presented. Luke explains how: "… although it was a difficult thing to raise funds for the trip to India, it is a journey that I will never forget."

Within the first year of their attendance at the Focus School, based on their strategic readings and figuring out what behaviour to adopt, the students settled into the new school environment. Despite describing themselves as 'settling in' and beginning to understand what was expected of them at the school, the students also describe the immense pressure they endured in order to perform well. This was due mainly to two specific factors. One factor was that the Focus School had threatened students who did not perform well in their initial tests that they would have to return to their former schools. The second factor was that the students felt that their former schools and their communities and families were watching to see if they would succeed. TK notes:

> Everybody's eyes were on me from Wolmarans. I could not let them down. I could not let myself down. I could not go back to my former school. Also ... my old school had faith in me. The principal believed in me. And my parents had aspirations for me to be an achiever. Also I wanted to be a pilot or an optician.

Mona discusses how other students had to leave the school and says that this motivated her to work hard, stating that: "I remember so many people left ... I wanted to be there, I did not want to be sent home."

The students also came to realise that in order to be successful at the school they had to be strategic in the social adaptations that they made. Mona describes how she understood that the choice of friends at the school was decisive in positioning her as an achieving student. On this issue, she points out that: "I only hung out with the students who were in the top ten and hardly ever got into trouble." Phumla notes that although she did not consider herself good at working in groups, she came to realise that to do well she needed to find ways to work with her peers in order to understand the work. Staying at the school made this easier and during the weekends she notes that it was much easier to study at the school than if she went home.

Not only were their peer socialisation practices important, the students also described how they realised that they needed to develop relationships with the teachers at the school as this positioned them as hard working students. Luke describes how he made an effort to endear himself to his teachers by always showing an interest in his learning, observing that: "I practically made a nuisance of myself asking the teachers to explain everything that I did not understand. The teachers liked me for that." Phumla notes that her Grade 11 Mathematics teacher in particular was instrumental in helping her improve her Mathematics mark and explains that: "Mr Gibbon was very helpful, offering help to us whenever we asked, usually it was at least once or twice a week after school that he would help us with our work."

Mona's realisation that she had been granted an exceptional educational opportunity for fulfilling her academic aspirations changed how she interacted with the school space. Although Mona was an introvert she realised that she had to make use of the resources available to her if she wanted to succeed. She described how she pushed herself out of her comfort zone to approach the teachers when she experienced difficulties with her work. She noted that the fact that the teachers were always willing to help assisted her to overcome her shyness in approaching them. Mona stated that over time she became more confident and was later invited to become a tutor to the Mathematics students in the lower grades.

Over time the students came to invest themselves in the new field environment and explained that they no longer wanted to return home at the weekends. When asked if she chose to go home for the weekends, Mona responded by saying:

> I actually enjoyed the Focus School. I would rather go home with my friend from school to Wolmarans [a rural town]. I went home with other students who became my friends.

Similarly, TK and Luke, who had previously missed their siblings when they had moved to the Focus School, also discuss how they chose to stay at the school over weekends: "I enjoyed socialising at the Focus School. I found that my friends from home had not seemed to move on as I had" (TK). Luke puts it as follows:

> Remember, I told you ... my friends that I left behind were not happy that I had 'deserted' them. Our relationship was not the same any more. The Focus School had become my haven ... away from the conflicts at home ... and where I was achieving much better results than ever before.

Investing in the new school field over time, the students came to embody the rules and regularities of the Focus School as their own. As their subjectivities were shifting and adapting they describe how they began to develop what Fataar (2015:113) describes as a 'thin connectedness' to their domestic environment and 'firmer attachments' to the new school field. They accomplished this over time via their investing in the new school field and the development of fluid and adaptive subjectivities, i.e. a trans-local habitus.

Establishment of a trans-local habitus at the Focus School

The students' mediation of their subjectivities via socialisation and development of social competencies, worked together to develop their fluid and adaptable subjectivities that enabled them to move towards cultivating a trans-local habitus. Furthermore, the students established a trans-local habitus which enabled them to become successful at the Focus School.

The idea of trans-local habitus builds on the idea of trans-nationalism. Trans-nationalism, in relation to individuals migrating to different or new locations, can be defined as "belonging to or organizing daily life between and among different locales that span borders" (Man & Cohen 2015:258). Trans-localism refers to individuals as they move within local boundaries from one location to another. Fataar (2015), in his work on young people's emerging subjectivities in relation to their school going in the post-apartheid urban landscape, refers to trans-localism as the shifting processes and adaptations that young people make as they move across the city spaces in order to access quality schooling. For the four students, developing a trans-local habitus required them to mentally and physically embody the requirements of the new school field. A trans-local habitus is therefore a habitus that incorporates a socio-spatial mobility which the students had embodied over time in order to become socially, geographically, culturally and linguistically integrated into the new social space or field. It is this integration, i.e. the cultivation of a trans-local habitus, that allowed the four students to gain access to the opportunities at the Focus School in order to realise their educational aspirations.

Using Bourdieu's analogy of 'playing the game', the students came to embody the rules and regulations of the new field environment that enabled them to develop a 'feel for the game' at the Focus School and begin to play the game successfully. This required them to conform to what was considered acceptable behaviour at the Focus School and learn to optimally utilise the resources that were available to them. TK started to improve his time management, stating that: "I had to get used to the fact that classes started on the first day of school at the Focus School." Luke realised that he would have to change his behaviour as the way he had behaved at his previous school would not be tolerated at the Focus School and reported that: "I was used to fooling around in class at my old school. I realised that this kind of behaviour was not going to get me anywhere." All four students realised the value of working with their peers and organised study groups that supported their learning. They also noted that they had to work harder than they ever did before. Mona describes how she learned to use the teachers as a resource to support her learning:

> I was not used to asking teachers for help because I am shy. But they were there … They were available … so I just had to be brave as it was for my own good … and ask for help.

These strategies were used by the students to shift their educational subjectivities in order to establish a trans-local habitus. Not only did the students shift and adapt their educational subjectivities at the Focus School, they realised that when they went home they needed to change how they engaged with education and their new learning practices when they were in their domestic space. Regarding this issue TK states that: "When I went home on the weekends and school holidays, I drew up a time table for studying and spent a lot of time with my school work."

These shifts and adaptations the students had made to their educational subjectivities were noted by their families and friends, with Luke noting that: "My friend in Pula could not understand why I was not fooling around with them anymore. They called me a nerd because I was sitting with my books more." Phumla describes how she now felt confident enough to support her siblings with their school work and reported that: "I used my skills that I had learnt at the Focus School to assist my siblings in their school work when I went home during the holidays." What this data illustrates is that the students had now embodied the shifts and changes in their educational subjectivities as seen in their ability to utilise the practices of the Focus School across different spaces.

My argument is, therefore, that by shifting their educational subjectivities via the socialisation practices in their new school field, they were able to develop social and educational competency that enabled them to cultivate a fluid and adaptable habitus, i.e. a trans-local habitus. Thus, a trans-local habitus can be described as a habitus that is successfully established through the weaving together of new practices across different spaces.

Conclusion

This chapter has placed as central to the research focus how the four high school students mediated their educational subjectivities at the Focus School in light of their mobility between their domestic environments and the school field. What is of interest, and could be considered in a further study, is whether the students were able to continue the shifts and adaptations they made in their educational subjectivities at the Focus School to another new field environment. Included in my interviews, the four respondents provided a brief discussion on their tertiary studies after their successful completion of Grade 12. This narrative shows that three of the students had embodied the changes they had made to their educational subjectivities, allowing them to continue to move successfully between multiple field environments. Here I define 'becoming successful' as the students' aspirations for their tertiary education and future careers. Of the four students, Luke and Mona established a desire to become mechanical engineers while studying at the Focus School. On completion of their Grade 12 studies they were accepted into a tertiary institution to study mechanical engineering. TK's aspiration was to become a pilot, however, while at the Focus School he realised that as he wore spectacles he would not qualify to study aviation. He therefore changed his career plans and chose to study dentistry. Phumla's initial aspiration was to become a doctor. During her Grade 12 year, due to her very good Mathematic results, she was awarded a bursary to study a Bachelor of Commerce (BCom) degree and was accepted at the University of Cape Town (UCT). This was strongly supported by her father and she decided to accept the bursary and shift her aspirations to study towards a BCom degree. She did not, however, complete the degree at UCT, leaving at the end of the first year to begin work at a bank. While working she enrolled to complete her studies through the University of South Africa (UNISA) on a part-time basis. She was (at the time of writing) working and completing her part-time studies.

The manner in which the four students were able to move beyond the Focus School to go on and become successful in their further studies, for me is an indication of their establishment of a successful trans-local habitus. For the four students in this study their ability to shift and adapt their educational subjectivities 'on the move', through the development of social competencies and fluid and adaptable subjectivities, and an embodiment of the 'sense of the game' in the new field environment, enabled them to become successful at the Focus School. A trans-local habitus, I argue therefore, is the ability to successfully shift and adapt one's subjectivity as one moves across different field contexts. In other words, a successful trans-local habitus is one that allows the individual, via their navigation across different field contexts, to successfully change or adapt their dispositions to the rules and regularities of the new field context.

References

Bourdieu P. 1977. *Outline of a Theory of Practice*. Cambridge University Press. https://doi.org/10.1017/CBO9780511812507

Bourdieu P. 1990. *The logic of practice*. Stanford: Stanford University Press.

Bourdieu P. 1998. *Practical Reason: On the Theory of Action*. Stanford: Stanford University Press.

Bourdieu P & Wacquant L. 1992. "The purpose of reflexive sociology (the Chicago workshop)". In: P Bourdieu & L Wacquant (eds). *An invitation to reflexive sociology*. Chicago: University of Chicago Press. 60–215.

Elkin F & Handel G. 1989. *The child and society: The process of socialization*. New York: McGraw-Hill.

Elliott A & Urry J. 2010. *Mobile lives*. New York: Routledge.

Fataar A. 2009. Schooling subjectivities across the post-apartheid city. *African Education Review*, 6(1):1–18. https://doi.org/10.1080/18146620902857202

Fataar A. 2015. *Engaging schooling subjectivities across post-apartheid urban spaces*. Stellenbosch: AFRICAN SUN MeDIA. https://doi.org/10.18820/9781920689834

Hillier J & Rooksby E. 2005. "Introduction to First Edition". In: J Hillier & E Rooksby (eds). *Habitus: A Sense of Place*. England: Ashgate. 19–42.

Levitt P. 2001. *The transnational villagers* (Volume 46). Berkeley: University of California Press.

Man G & Cohen R (eds). 2015. *Engendering Transnational Voices: Studies in Family, Work, and Identity*. Canada: Wilfrid Laurier University Press.

Oakes T & Schein L (eds). 2006. *Translocal China: Linkages, identities and the reimagining of space*. London: Taylor Francis Group.

Reay D. 2004. 'It's all becoming a habitus': beyond the habitual use of habitus in educational research. *British Journal of Sociology of Education*, 25(4):431–444. https://doi.org/10.1080/0142569042000236934

Webb J, Schirato T & Danaher G. 2002. *Understanding Bourdieu*. Crows Nest, NSW, Australia: Allen & Unwin.

Woodward K. 1997. *Identity and difference*. London: Sage.

Chapter 5

Negotiating belonging at school: High school girls' mediation of their out-of-classroom spaces

Elzahn Rinquest

Introduction

This chapter offers an understanding of how a group of high school girls mediated the toughness of belonging at school. Based on ethnographic research, I deliberately positioned myself in the girls' school-world in order to gain novel insight into how they lived and experienced their unique school context. The participants are a group of racially and culturally diverse Grade 10 girls from middle- to lower-middle-class families who formed connections with each other that entangled them in a peer network at school. Their school, Mount Valley High (pseudonym), is a private high school on the outskirts of Cape Town. This study specifically focuses on girls and not boys. The aim of this study is not to compare findings related to gender. This decision is guided by the acknowledgement that, apart from the biological differences, boys and girls view and react to physical settings differently as well as identify and resolve problems related to relationships, their personal space and privacy differently (Proshansky, Fabian & Kaminoff 1983). Additionally, recent studies have found that girls form 'natural peer groups' which "share patterns of beliefs, values, symbols and activities" (Adriaens 2014:104) more readily than boys do. The participants' *desire to belong* is viewed as a key element to how they went about making a 'place' for themselves while they collaboratively 'made place' at the school. I explore the complexity of the various spatial dimensions at this school (material, social and mental) and their role in producing the girls' unfolding subjectivities.

The post-apartheid South African context has seen issues of race, class, gender and language play out in unexpected ways. This is in part the consequence of overwhelming social realignments that have been taking place in the country. According to Fataar (2010), the transformation associated with the political transition has forced South African youth to find new ways of positioning and evaluating themselves as they are now situated in a "newer, more complex terrain" (Fataar 2010:44). In the light of these transformations, I argue that schools and other educational institutions are significant sites where a variety of cultures, languages, racial interactions and class manifestations connect and interact (see Vandeyar 2008). At my research site, Mount Valley High (pseudonym), I found that young people were constantly (re)organising and (re)positioning themselves in a struggle to find their own place at school.

Research focused on youth identities within school spaces are essential as they allow us "to highlight the importance of young people's experiences of education in the here and now, as well as having concern for education's future impacts, encouraging us to engage with young people as knowledgeable actors whose current and future lifeworlds are worthy of investigation" (Holloway, Hubbard & Pimlott-Wilson 2010:594). An understanding of how high school girls inhabit and identify with their school offers invaluable insights into how they come to construct and negotiate identities related to their school-going experiences and the school as a specific socialising institution. This enables various stakeholders to "respond more adequately to young people's uneven and complex immersions into their school going" (Fataar 2010:14).

High school girls are constantly engaged in complex interactions in the various informal spaces of their school. By acting in these spaces, they are actively involved in making place, a process which shapes and re-organises the spaces they move through. The nature and extent of the identifications that high school girls make emotionally, symbolically, as well as with the physical building and material spaces of their school, influence the social networks that they come to create. These identifications consequently guide the way that these students see themselves in relation to the physical and social spaces of their school, which contributes to the types of place-based identities they negotiate and establish for themselves. The interplay between the school as a specific place and the place-based identities of the students inhabiting it, suggests that places shape the people who inhabit them and vice versa.

The ethnographic study used to collect the data discussed in this chapter was limited to observing and interviewing a group of five Grade 10 girls. Selection criteria required that these girls should have formed part of a group of friends who spend their time together outside the formal classroom in the informal spaces of the school. As this was a qualitative research study, the interpretive method was employed to "yield insight and understandings of behavior, explain actions from the participant's perspective" (Scotland 2012:12). The aim was to produce data which "provides rich evidence and offers credible and justifiable accounts (internal validity/credibility)" (Scotland 2012:12).

In the six-month period that I conducted my fieldwork I spent the first month orientating myself and doing initial in-depth participant observations. This enabled me to acquaint myself with the functioning of the school and orientate myself accordingly; identify the informal spaces that I focused my observations on; informally observe behaviour in these informal spaces and (together with the principal and head of department) identify a group of Grade 10 girls who were to be the focus of my observations and interviews for the following five months. Time was also spent gathering the necessary consent forms and preparing the students for the intended research and their role as participants. Critical ethnography usually involves a substantial amount of interviewing and entails an extended period of participant observation in order to come to a deeper understanding of those being observed. I collected rich qualitative data by means of the following methods: participant observations; focus-group discussions; individual semi-structured interviews; photo-elicitation interviews and writing produced by the student participants.

My main analytical findings reveal that these girls focused on how they went about making place in ways that stretched across the three spatial dimensions (physical, social and mental), as well as how they went about this in individual, communal and strategic ways guided by their affective positions in response to the affectivity of the place. I argue that through the school's encouragement of the students to express themselves in the school's spaces, the students went on to inhabit and create the school as a place in unanticipated ways. In the school's 'out-of-sight' spaces the girls were emoting, acting, negotiating and strategising in order to establish their emerging identities. Importantly, the culture of the school opened up the space for these girls to act and their acting at school was instrumental in reorganising and transforming the school space. The school attempted to be an inclusive space that accommodated diversity, but the girls' affectivities, their bodies and their embodied dispositions, co-constituted the school as a specific type of place. I argue that the girls interpreted the culture of the school and acted in response to its discourses and their *desire to belong*, and consequently constructed ways of 'living' at the school. It became clear that the character of the school as a place was constantly lived, experienced and reordered by those who moved through it.

Theoretical considerations

The theoretical framework that I employ in this chapter seeks to lay a platform for analysing the struggles of teenage girls' mediation of their schooling terrain. The five girls, who are the focus of this chapter, negotiated their emerging identities while pursuing spaces to belong inside the school. I combine theories related to the production of space, the desire to belong, place-identity, place-making and affectivity to construct a unique lens that allowed me to observe the school-based lives of the five individual high school girls.

The framework is founded on a combination of Henri Lefebvre's production of space theory (1971/1991) and Proshansky, Fabian and Kaminoff's (1983) work on the formation of place-identities. Notions of space and place-based identities are thus combined to assist me in understanding the ways in which high school girls behaved in their out-of-classroom school spaces.

Lefebvre states that "[s]ocially lived space and time, socially produced, depends on physical and mental constructs" (Elden 2004:190). He notes that space is produced as a social formation and as a conception, a mental construction. From these ideas Lefebvre derives his conceptual triad of spatial practice in terms of which he views space in three ways: perceived, lived and conceived. Space is understood as a unity of physical, social and mental space (Lefebvre 1971/1991). Drawing on Lefebvre's (1971/1991) spatial theory, I suggest that school space is a coming together of all the various facets of the school environment and that a 'place' is a particular articulation of the interaction of these various spatial dimensions (Massey 1994). A 'place' can therefore never be a fixed, static and stable entity that portrays a singular, permanent meaning. Understanding the students' mediation of the spaces outside of their classrooms includes examining its materiality in relation to the ways in which the students inhabited, interacted with and moved through the different spaces. McGregor (2004a) argues that schools are built and organised in order to produce particular social interactions; therefore physical space becomes integral to the specific social relations that occur within the school environment.

Social processes transform and rearrange the social space of the school. The inhabitants are thus active participants in a process of 'making place'. This place-making entails activities which I refer to as 'place-making practices'. These place-making practices incorporate interactive social behaviours and they focus, for example, on how the students form peer-affiliations, arrange themselves in groups and congregate in, and claim, specific spaces. I suggest that people attach meaning to, and identify with a place whilst engaged in complex individual and communal interactions to achieve a 'making of place' (Marcouyeux & Fleury-Bahi 2011). People are, therefore, constructors of place where place-making is a consequence of their everyday interactions within a complexity of networks and intersections in their lived school spaces (Nespor 1997).

Driven by the desire to belong (Allen & Bowles 2012), each individual forms strong or weak connections with the various aspects of their school space. Students inevitably connect emotions to experiences in the various spatial dimensions at school and derive meaning from what they perceive a place to be. The data-based discussion in this chapter highlights how the experiences of individuals in specific moments in place are multiple, varied and dependent on how the individual is situated inside of, or in relation to, the flows and frictions that co-construct place (Massey 1994). The desire to belong is a prominent motivator of everyday human interaction which affects and guides behaviour and emotions (Allen & Bowles 2012). For adolescent girls, the struggles to belong in school thus plays an important role in their negotiation of place (or school-based) identities, influencing the ways in which they mediate the spaces of their school.

Complex patterns of cognition are forged in relation to specifics of school space, where "conscious and unconscious ideas, feelings, values, goals, preferences, skills, meanings, and behavioural tendencies" (Marcouyeux & Fleury-Bahi 2011:345) converge. I argue that "[t]he individual builds place identity to the extent that he or she feels attached to it" (Marcouyeux & Fleury-Bahi 2011:346). Thus, for an individual to willingly maintain a relationship with a specific place, a link needs to be created through a process of identifying with, and constructing an attachment to, the specific place (Hidalgo & Hernandez 2001).

I expand on the theory of place-making by emphasising the concept of affect as a decisive dimension involved in the place-making process (see Zembylas 2003, 2005, 2007, 2015). The concept of affect can be viewed as the driving force behind a 'chain of events' that takes place when bodies encounter each other inside a school. I understand affect as created through its preceding encounters and interactions, and accumulated within the girls' bodies. Also, affect is viewed as a continuous process where ongoing encounters continue to influence and shape the affectivity of the girls' bodies. Importantly, because affect circulates and is transmitted between bodies and 'affects' bodies, it continues to evolve (Mulcahy 2012). The affective embodiment of individuals shifts as they encounter emotions and the reactions of other people, which in turn shape the affective position of the person. Thus, affect is not static; it is always in process. I argue that during this process of affective place-making each individual constructs a unique sense of that place and of their individual identities in relation to that place (Altman & Low 1992; Hidalgo & Hernandez 2001).

Fundamentally, student-school interactions lead to the formation of a specific sense of the school environment, which leads the student to form specific kinds of attachments to the school (Altman & Low 1992; Hidalgo & Hernandez 2001). People-place relationships are described through the place attachments and identifications they make with the places they encounter. The nature and extent of the attachments that students form within their school, and the extent to which they choose to identify with the school, emphasise the affective processes that are entangled in each student's school-going and identity negotiations (see Fataar 2009). The process of affective place-making in this study thus involves the five participants' social interactions, emotional responses, the actions they take in order to position themselves among their peers, as well as their reactions to their encounters with the mental, physical and social elements of school. I argue that all these practices work together to construct the process of affective place-making to produce a unique and particular place for each of the selected girls at the school.

Methodology

This chapter is based on my ethnographic immersion in a high school over a period of six months. As an ethnographer I adopted an involved, connected observer stance and immersed myself in the everyday world of high school girls for these six months. The aim was to gain a greater understanding of the girls' lives at school. This approach allowed me, to some extent, to gain 'insider' status in this context. In order to become an accepted and trusted individual by the participants, I had to achieve "shared, social and situated ways of being with participants" (Hobson 2005:127). I therefore involved myself in all of the students' activities at school. In this way, I could share in the situations which these students were engaged in and could experience some of the textures of the social context of their school for myself. During my time at the school I took extensive field notes which involved accounts of events, records of conversations based on unstructured interviews, and impressions of how the student participants responded to particular social events or activities. During the first few weeks at the school I built relationships with the participating students in order to establish a level of trust between myself and the selected participants. These relationships formed the interactive basis for the focus-group discussions and semi-structured individual interviews.

Five data-collection methods were utilised: (1) participant observations, which are valuable because "implicit features in social life are more likely to be revealed as a result of the observer's continued presence and because of the observer's ability to observe behaviour rather than just rely on what is said" (Bryman 2001:328); (2) unstructured and semi-structured interviews which formed an integral part of the ethnographic research as it generated insight into the interviewees' points of view; (3) focus-group discussions which encouraged the participants to develop and articulate their thoughts and enabled them "to develop ideas collectively, bringing forward their own priorities and perspectives" (Smithson 2009:359); (4) photo-elicitation interviews utilising student-produced photographs which were used as a stimulus during the interview in order to "trigger responses and memories and unveil participants' attitudes, views, beliefs, and meanings" (Meo 2010:150); and (5) photo diaries were a final addition to the data-collection method. Participants attached reflective thoughts to a selection of photographs of school spaces and considered their emotional responses to the activities that took place in these different spaces. These served as thought-generating stimuli for reflection on their actions in the informal spaces of school.

The utilisation of a qualitative, ethnographic research approach based on these five data-collection methods allowed me to generate thick and in-depth data. The data allowed me to develop an understanding of high school girls' complex mediation of their school spaces while negotiating their own identities as part of a complex process of 'making place'.

Living the materiality of school

How the girls live the material conditions of their school was integral to the ways in which they negotiated their place identities at school. Significantly, the participating girls did not choose to attend Mount Valley High as their first choice of high school. They each negotiated a circuitous educational path that 'ended them up' at this specific site. As I learned more about the girls' realities, it became clear that the struggles they experienced in their school journeys mainly stemmed from a pressing desire – the need to belong. Each of the five girls had attended more than two public schools, some as many as five schools, prior to their arrival at the school. Mount Valley High is a private institution, embodying a particular *expressive culture* based on its stated aim of actively promoting inclusiveness. This culture received and positioned each girl distinctly at the school.

The school is situated in a peri-urban suburb of Cape Town next to a national road in a farm-like setting with many plant-rich outdoor spaces and scattered classroom structures. This setting provides a favourable locale for the school's open and relaxed expressive culture. The term 'expressive culture' is used by Bernstein, Elvin and Peters (1966:429) to describe the activities, procedures and judgements involved in the school's production and transmission of its values and norms, which, in turn, are the sources of the school's shared identity and cohesiveness. In this light, Mount Valley High exhibited a highly inclusive expressive culture that was evident in its daily operations. This was the consequence of the school's emphasis on an open and relaxed school ethos, flexible physical arrangements, and the availability of supportive resources. It was this perception of Mount Valley High, as an environment that accommodates a diverse group of students and encourages their uniqueness, in comparison to the strictly regulated public high schools in the community, that made this particular school an attractive option for the girls.

Emily, a cheerful white girl, struggled academically at the neighbouring public school due to the large class groups, the fast pace of school work, and the overall academic pressure that she felt the school placed on her. She sought out the remedial support that the teachers and small class groups at Mount Valley High could offer her.

Lulu is a polite and conscientious black girl from a stable family. Being new at the school, she often expressed a longing for the familiarity of her previous high school, her friends there and the dance classes that she had left behind. Lulu has a passion for dance. Her ambition to pursue dance as a career path was, however, shattered when she learnt that her parents were sending her to Mount Valley High which does not offer dance as a subject. Although Lulu did not entirely resent attending her new school, she struggled to form social connections which made her transition a challenging process.

Ariya, a cavalier white girl, attended the same public school as Emily. Ariya got into fights with other girls, displayed disruptive behaviour and generally felt out of place at her previous school. She describes her so-called deviant behaviour as the result of built-up anger stemming from emotional trauma related to her parents' divorce, her rejection of her mother and the recent death of her father. Her aunts' search for a safe educational space for Ariya led them to choose Mount Valley High for her as a desperate last resort.

Hannah is a talkative and energetic coloured girl. Her father lives abroad but provides for the family's financial needs. He believes that his children must attend private schools because, according to him, these schools deliver better education. He visits South Africa once a year and has not established a fatherly relationship with Hannah. Hannah lives with her mother and two brothers. Her mother does not work and spends most of her day at home. Her mother's lifestyle includes excessive use of alcohol which leads to regular verbal fights between herself and Hannah. Hannah's mother generally plays a non-supportive role in her life.

Ashley is an assertive and sociable girl. She lives with her mother and stepfather in a security complex five minutes away from school. Her biological father remarried several times and has numerous children from these marriages. Ashley goes as far as describing her family set-up as 'dysfunctional'; however, her home environment seems safe and stable.

These five girls each had personal reasons for coming to Mount Valley High. They connected with each other at the school and went on to establish a peer network. Their diverse domestic backgrounds influenced them in choosing this particular school. The girls' family lives and their experiences in their previous schools positioned their behaviour and actions in specific ways, both individually and in groups at the school.

Their navigation of place was central to their group dynamics and the identifications that they made in light of their place-making. I suggest that the nature of the girls' mediation of, and assimilation into, the school culture depended on *who* they were, *where* they came from and *how* they went about establishing their identifications.

Socio-spatial positioning

Heterogeneous experiences of schooling brought the girls to Mount Valley High and situated each of them inside its locales in different ways. Regardless of their schooling situation these girls went about establishing their capacity to mediate their world while remaining committed to the processes of learning and schooling. The ways the girls mediated the physical, social and mental dimensions of their schooling space explains their socio-spatial positioning at school. The girls utilised school spaces and resources away from the gaze of teachers and other adults in personal, needs-driven and diverse ways. The need to acquire social status and power amongst their peers were noticeable elements that guided the social behaviour of the girls. This was done either through asserting a harsh localised dominance that conveyed a social position of power through creating the idea of belonging to the 'cool' peer group or by adopting strategic place-based practices that enabled them to establish a larger peer network. While Ariya remained relatively rooted in one space, asserting her dominance in this way, Hannah networked and moved around the school which allowed her to establish social contact with a variety of peers whom she deemed important in order to create her social dominance.

The girls demonstrated that social acceptance and assertion can be accomplished in various ways at school. Ariya and Hannah found unique ways of constructing and maintaining peer networks that led to them becoming embedded in the school, each in their distinct ways and driven by their personal needs. Their socio-spatial practices enabled them to form a particular type of attachment to the school, which led to them expressing strong place-based identifications. They both expressed 'feeling at home' since attending Mount Valley High. This is understood as an expression of their desire for acceptance, belonging and social security – something that both these girls were not experiencing at home. Their expression of feelings of self-worth and personal value during interviews demonstrated how their experiences of the physical and social aspects at school influenced their cognition of the place that they define Mount Valley High to be.

The girls' ways of identifying with their school can be categorised by drawing on Nespor (1997) and Breakwell's (1986, 1992, 1993) theorisation of people's interactions with space. By utilising Nespor's lenses of 'emplacement' and 'displacement', the girls' place-making practices and place-based identifications in the out-of-classroom spaces at school can be categorised. Young people who connect with the school space, such as Ariya and Hannah, can be categorised as embedded or 'emplaced', and those who struggle to make meaningful connections to space or are 'displaced from comfortable space' can be categorised as being 'displaced' (Nespor 1997).

Emily, Lulu and Ashley saw themselves as detached from the space, merely passing through the school space, not connecting to the school's material and social spaces at any deep level, or allowing social spaces to influence their identities or transform them in any way. They were rather yearning to form strong connections to different spaces in which they felt 'embedded' (Nespor 1997).

Lulu preferred to establish peer affiliations cautiously and rarely spoke of her associations with the school; she did, however, refer to her previous school and friends whom she yearned for. Lulu eventually established her belonging in a single-raced group of black girls which evoked racialised reactions from the other girls. Emily, in her struggle to establish connections with her peers, would at times prefer the solitude of her phone conversations in private spaces that she carved out for herself. She regularly expressed her dissatisfaction with the school's lack of an extramural programme which she felt she could benefit from. Ashley and Hannah both enjoyed the company of a variety of students and as such became mobile place-makers. Ashley, in particular, conveyed an awareness of the bodily and social adaptations that she made as she moved through the school spaces in order to connect to and identify with certain peers. She also often expressed a feeling of superiority in relation to the type of school that Mount Valley High is, and as such her non-identification lead to her 'displacement'.

Positive place-based identifications that the girls made seemed partially to be a consequence of the interaction between their personal histories connected to their domestic lifeworlds, and their previous schooling experiences that were entangled with the behaviours that the expressive culture of the school allowed for. Mount Valley High thus became a place that was instrumental in responding to the girls' personal needs for belonging and acceptance, and as such offered respite from the social void they experienced in their domestic environments. Evidently, even though both girls (Hannah and Ariya) formed positive attachments with the school, they did so in diverse ways, illustrating how place-making is an individualised process that is unique for each person.

The act of successfully claiming ownership of their school spaces ensured Hannah and Ariya's sense of belonging in that space and therefore they could utilise it in whichever way they chose in order to express and negotiate their identities individually as well as communally. Instead of feeling disconnected and merely passing through space, it was possible for them to connect to the material and social spaces of school at a deeper level through imagining school as a place that felt like home. And in so doing, the girls allowed the school spaces to influence their personal identifications, and as such, extended and transformed them (Nespor 1997).

From the analysis above it is evident that schools as socialising institutions are "important social contexts in which to examine the social construction of adolescent identities as students in these settings are caught up in self-defining struggles located primarily in their relations with their peers" (Wilkinson & Pearson 2013:180). The everyday practice of schooling is therefore "constructed out of particular interactions and mutual articulations of social relations, social processes, experiences and understandings" (McGregor 2004:47). It is evident that the interactions and articulations that occur between people within the school space create experiences and construct understandings. The social relationships people construct within schools contribute to the identifications and attachments they make to school as a place (Hollingworth & Archer 2010:597). The toughest part is the mediation of the educational landscape in pursuit of belonging to some form of school or schooling.

Mediating the toughness of belonging at school

The participating girls interpreted the culture of their school and acted in response to its discourses by utilising a combination of individual, group and strategic *affective* place-making practices, turning the school into a particular place. Their place-making processes started with each girl's affective positioning, which was embedded in a fusion of their history, family, culture, language and race, as well as their previous experiences with schooling. Each girl's affect was enacted through emotional responses to particular social encounters, which in turn elicited actions and reactions. The ways in which each girl chose to act and react to such encounters in turn guided the formation of her place identifications and attachments at school.

Firstly, the girls acted individually at school by positioning themselves in relation to their peers. When one girl was harsh towards another less dominant peer this approach not only produced her harshness and dominance and superior positioning, but simultaneously produced the other's lesser status. The harsh girl acted in this manner as a response to the culture established by the dominant peer group. Marked by rudeness, this group produced an assimilative culture which attached itself strongly to the school and simultaneously worked to detach others from this particular place. This culture strongly attached the girls who were assertive – and in this case, rude and rebellious – to the school, and thereby served to distance and alienate those who were less assertive.

Secondly, the participating girls positioned themselves at school through the establishment of groups. One such incident portrayed the girls' affective positioning in relation to their understanding and embodiment of race. This incident displayed how groups gave 'meaning' to the school through their use of race as an organiser of relations. Racialised behaviour was transmitted by some of the girls through the strategic and calculated use of language and labels in order to position and organise themselves socially on the school terrain. Race at the school had become a function of social positioning which informed the ways in which the students organised and categorised each other into groups against the backdrop of a seemingly deracialised school environment. Despite its official culture of inclusivity, Mount Valley High became re-racialised through the behaviour of its students inside its school spaces (see also Dolby 2001). This incident shows how both the students and the school as a place were repositioned by the racialised place-making practices of the girls.

Thirdly, the students asserted themselves individually by mobilising the available structures at the school. This strategic form of place-making should be understood as a careful consideration of the environment and the subsequent strategic utilisation and mobilisation of the available structures in order to influence how the school functions as a 'place'. Through this process of making place, a confident and assertive, yet weakly positioned girl, could through her assertiveness and strategic use of space, gain power over those who deemed themselves as the 'powerful'. This emphasises how one can make a 'place' work for oneself when approaching it strategically. Mount Valley High became a place where students invoked their agency by making the school's structures and discourses work for them as part of their own positioning practices.

The girls' affective dispositions came into play when their bodies collided with others inside the school. This 'collision of affects' had a way of organising and positioning the girls inside the school spaces and consequently made the school something other than what it was before the 'collision'. This in turn led to the ongoing processes of positioning and repositioning where the girls' affect, *as product*, influenced each other and as something *in process* continued to be influenced by the environment and thus continually evolving. Importantly, the girls' affective orientation evolved and positioned them in specific ways, contributing to how they were creating and recreating the character of the place. The culture of the school was therefore co-established by the interaction of the affectivities drawn out by the person-person/people-environment interactions taking place.

The school expresses a unique culture which is experienced and interpreted by each of its students. Each individual student exists and encompasses an embodied student identity which is constructed through previous interactions with schooling and influenced by domestic socialisations. When the school's expressive culture meets and interacts with the students a relationship emerges and a bond is established. The students go about shaping their attachments to the school on a continuum between embedded and detached, a process which is informed by their need to belong, a need not satisfied in other spaces of their lifeworlds. Consequently, a specific identity is forged and a particular place is made in an ongoing 'making of place'. Nothing and nobody stands still; they are always in the process of becoming.

Once the girls orientated themselves to the school's culture, their ways of acting at school were informed by the nature of their place identifications and the extent of their attachments to the school. The girls all conveyed a need to belong, desiring to be accepted by one or more of their peers at school and wanting to belong *at* school. The girls who aligned themselves with peers who identified closely with the culture of the school found a sense of belonging not only amongst their chosen peers, but the school and its affectivities. The inclusive, supportive and relatively non-judgemental expressive culture of the school allowed some of the participants to express their uniqueness and opened up spaces for them to test other experimental identities. Some of the girls identified with the expressive culture of the school because this enabled them to make more distinct or unique place identifications. The school's inclusive culture provided a distinctive 'lifestyle' to which some of the girls could connect strongly. In contra-distinction to such identification, other girls experienced feelings of shame and embarrassment. These girls often expressed their desire to go to a 'normal' school in order to not be frowned upon by their peers from the surrounding public schools. Instead of using their placement as a form of self-identification, they preferred to present themselves as distinct or apart from the school's identity. Both of these groups of girls seemed to "use a place-related self-referent in order to present themselves as distinct from others" (Twigger-Ross & Uzzell 1996:207).

The girls' place identifications were also subject to how their experiences at school influenced their self-esteem. Some girls used the place of school to create a sense of worth and social value (Korpela 1989) that propelled them outside of their domestic life world into a world where they could reimagine themselves, repositioning themselves through the place identifications that they established at school. The qualities of the place of school in essence enabled these girls to boost their self-esteem (Twigger-Ross & Uzzell 1996). Conversely, some of the girls' responses to the school illustrated the undesirable effects that the school as a place, had on their self-esteem. When a student could not establish a place of belonging at school, feelings of isolation and rejection caused negative self-esteem associations and served to detach these girls from the school. The nature of the girls' place identifications better explains the extent to which they formed their attachments to the school. And additionally, the extent of the girls' attachments and detachments to the school became instrumental in understanding their place-making process.

These high school girls connected to the school along a continuum of 'firmly attached' on the one end to 'unattached' or 'detached' on the other. The school's expressive culture benefited some students more than others. The more assertive girls became dominant amongst their peers. Fundamentally, their student-school interactions led to the formation of a specific sense of the school environment, which in turn led the students to form specific kinds of attachments to the school.

Conclusion

I offer the metaphor 'finding a place to belong' as an attempt to capture the nature of the mediation practices or place-making of the five high school girls. The desire to belong operates as a backdrop to the girls' practices in the informal spaces of their school and consequently assists in gauging the extent to which they make place. The assimilative culture of the school provided the girls with a platform to exercise their place-making. They utilised the culture of the school, claimed spaces outside of their classrooms, and shaped these spaces through their practices in them. They transformed these spaces into a significant place. The extent of their place-making depended on the level of their assertiveness, and the assertiveness of their place-making depended on the extent to which they felt the need to belong, which is a desire that they attempted to fulfil in the spaces of their school.

Places such as schools should therefore be viewed as bearers of affect, which give rise to emotions, action and reactions, leading to affectivities that co-constitute the discursive environment as well as the practices that emerge in everyday contingent circumstances in the different spaces of the school. Schools are places where bodies collide, engage and establish identifications. The making of a place is a process that occurs through the complex interactions of all its inhabitants, but the construction and interpretation of that place rests with each individual. Place is therefore in the eye of the beholder. In other words, the school was a personal and individualised place for each of the five girls. Ultimately, what became apparent was that the girls were thinking all the time, and that their interactions at school were entangled in their practices of negotiating the process of becoming young adults and thereby finding and making their place in the world.

The chapter has sought to inform the way in which we understand the learning subject in diversified South African schools. In addition to our understanding of students' formal learning practices, I encourage a consideration of their movements and interactions in the school's out-of-classroom spaces which interact with and facilitate their learning. Key to this is youth subject-making in the context of current day South Africa and the struggles of young people over belonging and identification in a complex global-local world where their domains are complexly wired. I wish to encourage a reflexive positionality that acknowledges students as relatively autonomous mediating agents who reorganise and transform their educational environment through which they move daily.

References

Adriaens F. 2014. 'Diaspora girls doing identities': Creating ideal television programmes and narratives of the self. *European Journal of Cultural Studies*, 17(2):101–117. https://doi.org/10.1177/1367549413508096

Altman I & Low S. 1992. *Place attachment*. New York: Plenum. https://doi.org/10.1007/978-1-4684-8753-4

Allen KA & Bowles T. 2012. Belonging as a Guiding Principle in the Education of Adolescents. *Australian Journal of Educational & Developmental Psychology*, 12:108–119.

Bernstein B, Elvin H & Peters R. 1966. Ritual and Education. *Philosophical Transactions of the Royal Society of London*, 251:429–436. https://doi.org/10.1098/rstb.1966.0029

Breakwell GM. 1986. *Coping with Threatened Identity*. London: Methuen.

Breakwell GM. 1992. "Processes of self-evaluation: Efficacy and estrangement". In: GM Breakwell (ed). *Social Psychology of Identity and the Self-concept*. London: Surrey University Press. 35–55.

Breakwell GM. 1993. "Integrating paradigms: Methodological implications". In: GM Breakwell & DV Canter (eds). *Empirical Approaches to Social Representations*. Oxford: Clarendon Press. 180–201.

Bryman A. 2001. Interviewing in qualitative research. *Social Research Methods*. Oxford: Open University Press. 10–32.

Dolby N. 2001. *Constructing Race: Youth, Identity, and Popular Culture in South Africa*. Albany, NY: State University of New York Press.

Elden S. 2004. *Understanding Henri Lefebvre: Theory and the Possible*. London and New York: Continuum.

Fataar A. 2009. Schooling subjectivities across the post-apartheid city. *Africa Education Review*, 6(1):1–18. https://doi.org/10.1080/18146620902857202

Fataar A. 2010. "A pedagogy of hope in the 'capacity to aspire': Youth subjectivity across the post-apartheid schooling landscape". Inaugural address: Stellenbosch University.

Hidalgo MC & Hernandez B. 2001. Place attachment: Conceptual and empirical questions. *Journal of Environmental Psychology*, 21(3):273–281. https://doi.org/10.1006/jevp.2001.0221

Hobson D & Titchen A. 2005. "Phenomenology". In: B Somekh & C Lewin (eds). *Research Methods in the Social Sciences*. SAGE Publications. 121–130.

Hollingworth S & Archer L. 2010. Urban schools as urban places: School reputation, children's identities and engagement with education in London. *Urban Studies*, 47(3):584–603. https://doi.org/10.1177/0042098009349774

Holloway SL, Hubbard P, Jöns H & Pimlott-Wilson H. 2010. Geographies of education and the significance of children, youth and families. *Progress in Human Geography*, 34(5):583–600. https://doi.org/10.1177/0309132510362601

Korpela KM. 1989. Place identity as a product of environmental self regulation. *Journal of Environmental Psychology*, 9:241–256. https://doi.org/10.1016/S0272-4944(89)80038-6

Lefebvre H. 1971/1991. *The production of space*. Oxford, UK: Blackwell Publishers.

Marcouyeux A & Fleury-Bahi G. 2011. Place-Identity in a School Setting: Effects of the Place Image. *Environment and Behavior*, 43(3):344–362. https://doi.org/10.1177/0013916509352964

Massey D. 1994. *Space, place, and gender*. Minneapolis: University of Minnesota Press.

McGregor J. 2004a. Editorial. *Forum*, 46:2–5. https://doi.org/10.2304/forum.2004.46.1.4

Meo A. 2010. Picturing Student's Habitus: The Advantages and Limitations of Photo-Elicitation Interviewing in a Qualitative Study in the City of Buenos Aires. *International Journal of Qualitative Methods*, 9(2):149–171. https://doi.org/10.1177/160940691000900203

Mulcahy D. 2012. Affective assemblages: body matters in the pedagogic practices of contemporary school classrooms. *Pedagogy, Culture & Society*, 20(1):9–27. https://doi.org/10.1080/14681366.2012.649413

Nespor J. 1997. *Tangled up in school: politics, space, bodies, and signs in the educational process*. New Jersey: Lawrence Erlbaum.

Proshansky HM, Fabian AK & Kaminoff R. 1983. Place-identity: Physical world socialization of the self. *Journal of Environmental Psychology*, 3(1):57–83. https://doi.org/10.1016/S0272-4944(83)80021-8

Scotland J. 2012. Exploring the philosophical underpinnings of research: Relating ontology and epistemology to the methodology and methods of the scientific, interpretive, and critical research paradigms. *English Language Teaching*, 5(9): 9–16. https://doi.org/10.5539/elt.v5n9p9

Smithson J. 2009. "Focus Groups". In: P Alasuutari, L Brickman & J Brannen (eds). *Social Research Methods*. Los Angeles: Sage. 130–140.

Twigger-Ross C & Uzzell D. 1996. Place and Identity Processes. *Journal of Environmental Psychology*, 16:205–220. https://doi.org/10.1006/jevp.1996.0017

Vandeyar S. 2008. Shifting selves: The emergence of new identities in South African schools. *International Journal of Educational Development*, 28(3):286–299. https://doi.org/10.1016/j.ijedudev.2007.05.001

Wilkinson L & Pearson J. 2013. High School Religious Context and Reports of Same-Sex Attraction and Sexual Identity in Young Adulthood. *Social Psychology Quarterly*, 76(2):180–202. https://doi.org/10.1177/0190272513475458

Zembylas M. 2003. Emotions and Teacher Identity: A poststructural perspective. *Teachers and Teaching*, 9(3):213–238. https://doi.org/10.1080/13540600309378

Zembylas M. 2005. Discursive practices, genealogies, and emotional rules: A poststructuralist view on emotion and identity in teaching. *Teaching and Teacher Education*, 21(8):935–948. https://doi.org/10.1016/j.tate.2005.06.005

Zembylas M. 2007. The specters of bodies and affects in the classroom: a rhizo-ethological approach. *Pedagogy, Culture & Society*, 15(1):19–35. https://doi.org/10.1080/14681360601162030

Zembylas M. 2015. Rethinking race and racism as technologies of affect: theorizing the implications for anti-racist politics and practice in education. *Race Ethnicity and Education*, 18(2):145–162. https://doi.org/10.1080/13613324.2014.946492

Chapter 6

First generation disadvantaged students' mediation practices in the uneven 'field' of a South African university

Najwa Norodien-Fataar

Introduction

This chapter focuses on the mediation practices of first generation disadvantaged students at a university. It provides an account of the interaction between students' practices and the field conditions of their university. Drawing on qualitative data collected over an eighteen-month period, this chapter focuses on findings from seven purposively selected students. I discuss how these students are able to construct and develop mediation practices for their educational engagement at the university. The analysis that I offer is informed by Bourdieu's "logic of practice" with attendant concepts of field, hysteresis, capital, which I employ to examine the nature of the students' mediation practices. The focus is on their engagement in the formal teaching and learning spaces of the university as well as their informal engagement with peers, ICTs, and linguistic and concept acquisition strategies. The main argument that I proffer in this chapter is that the students adopt a particular type of mediation practice, based on what I call a 'logic of educational engagement' in respect of which they establish a viable educational path under trying circumstances.

Three aspects of the extant literature on disadvantaged students at university situate the focus of the chapter. The first highlights the importance of students' responsibilities and commitments to the university, and the practices that help them enhance their engagement at university (Bozalek 2009; Strydom 2009; Kuh 2009). A second aspect focuses on what institutions may do to optimise the educational experiences of their students (see Bitzer 2009; Makgoba 1997; Smit 2012; Van Schalkwyk 2009). These studies highlight universities' under-preparedness and inadequacy in providing students with a supportive and intellectually engaging platform for their university study. What is stressed here is the significant role that successful integration plays in disadvantaged students' social and academic adapatation during their studies. A third aspect discusses how students deal with constraining and enabling conditions at university (see Cross & Atinde 2014; Kapp, Badenhorst, Bangeni, Craig, Janse van

Rensburg, Le Roux, Prince, Pym & Van Pletzen 2014; Marshall & Case 2010; Mckay & Devlin 2014; Smit 2012). These studies emphasise a different, more productive way of thinking about disadvantaged students in higher education by focusing on the way in which the intellectual and cultural resources that they possess are beneficial to their studies.

Following from these perspectives, I identified the need to understand how these students mobilise their resources and forms of social and cultural capital to engage in their university education. I adopted a qualitative research approach for the study on which this chapter is based by using semi-structured interviews and focus-group discussions to obtain data on the selected students' university engagement practices. Based on this data, the chapter presents an argument around the forms of 'capital' that the students bring with them to the university and how they use these to respond to the challenges and opportunities that they encounter during their studies. I shall argue that they go on to build embodied learning practices in response to their reception and positioning at the university. These practices enable them to develop strategic engagement dispositions in respect of which they go on to engender academic success.

Bourdieu's logic of practice

Bourdieu's (1992) "logic of practice" and attendant concepts of capital, field, habitus and hysteresis are used to discuss how students develop and construct their educational engagement at the university. Bourdieu provides a broad view of the concept of capital by "employing a wider system of exchanges whereby assets of different kinds are transformed and exchanged within complex networks or circuits within and across fields" (Moore 2014:99). Thus, he conceptualises the notion of 'capital' not only as economic exchange, but also in terms of other forms of capital such as social and cultural capital. Bourdieu (2006) suggests that different types of capital exist in three forms. The first is the objectified state, in the form of cultural goods such as paintings, books, machines. The second is the embodied state, which includes the dispositions of the mind and body, and physical features such as language, stances, intonation and lifestyle choices. The third form of capital is the institutionalised state that exists in the form of educational qualifications (Bourdieu 2006). Moore (2014:103) indicates that the third expression of capital is in the form of habitus "which does not have a material existence in itself in the world" since it (habitus) "includes attitudes and dispositions but known only through its realizations in practice" (Moore 2014:103).

Bourdieu first developed the concept of cultural capital to explain the disparity between children from different social classes when they participate in schooling. As he explains:

> The notion of cultural capital initially presented itself to me, in the course of research, as a theoretical hypothesis which made it possible to explain the unequal scholastic achievement of children originating from the different social classes by relating academic success, i.e. the specific profits which children from the different classes and class fractions can obtain in the academic market, to the distribution of cultural capital between the classes and class fractions.   (2006:106)

This perspective is grounded in Bourdieu's basic argument that the cultural capital of different social groups is unevenly valued. He explains that the value placed on any particular form of cultural capital is arbitrary – that is, it "cannot be deduced from any universal principle, whether physical, biological or spiritual" (Bourdieu & Passeron 1977:8). He argues that cultural capital is not naturally acquired but is arbitrarily formed, and that the cultural capital of the middle class has a higher status than that of the working class. Giving more value to one group over another creates conflict and points of struggle among the different social class groups in the social world.

Using the notion of cultural capital, Bourdieu sought to move away from the view that academic success or failure is the result of natural aptitude. He also challenged the economistic view that regarded monetary investments as a determinant of success. For Bourdieu, an economistic view fails to take into account "the best hidden and socially most determinant educational investment" – that is, the domestic transmission of cultural capital (Bourdieu 2006:107). Bourdieu (2006) gives credence to the family as a source in which cultural capital is created. He argues that what is perceived as natural 'ability' or 'talent' is actually the product of an investment of time and cultural capital by the family.

According to Bourdieu and Wacquant (1992), capital functions as power in a field and the more capital an individual can acquire, the more power he or she will be able to exercise in the field. Bourdieu understands 'field' in terms of social rather than geographical or territorial spaces (Lingard 2013:9). This concept of field as a theoretical tool offers an "epistemological and methodological approach to a historicized and particular understanding of the social life" (Thomson 2014:79). This means that the concept of field allows researchers to "translate practical problems into empirical observations" (Thomson 2014:79). The field in my study is the social space which is made up of the university's educational support platform, which includes the courses that the selected students are registered for, the teaching and learning support services, and other support services at the university.

According to Jenkins (1992:52), a field is defined by:

> ... the stakes which are at stake – cultural goods (life-style), housing, intellectual distinction (education), employment, land, power (politics), social

class, prestige or whatever – and may be of differing degrees of specificity and concreteness. Each field, by virtue of its defining content, has a different logic and taken-for-granted structure of necessity and relevance which is both the product and producer of the habitus which is specific and appropriate to the field.

Bourdieu compares the field to a game and argues that field is "competitive with various agents using different strategies to improve or maintain their position" (Thomson 2014:67). I show in this chapter how the students counter-position themselves at the university and employ strategies to engage in their education. Bourdieu and Wacquant (1992) compared the field to a game guided by rules according to which various players take up particular field positions. These positions in the game determine the nature and quality of their actions. However, "in contrast to the rigidity of the game system, the field is much more fluid and complex than any game that one might ever design" (Bourdieu & Wacquant 1992:104). Bourdieu suggests that different fields and states exist and that each field contains "historically constituted areas of activity with their specific institutions and their own laws of functioning" (Bourdieu 1990:87). Thomson (2014:67) describes the nature of fields as "shaped differently according to the game that is played on them. They have their own rules, histories, star players, legends and lore". These fields or areas of activity are each "quite peculiar social worlds where the universal is engendered" (Bourdieu 1998:71). Jenkins (1992:53) points out that "the field is the crucial mediating context wherein external factors – changing circumstances – are brought to bear upon individual practice and institutions".

Bourdieu (1990, 1992) introduces 'habitus' as a related concept to understand human actions in relation to the 'field conditions'. He defines an individual's habitus as "ways of standing, speaking, walking, and thereby of feeling and thinking" and adds that habitus "refers to something historical, it is linked to individual history" (Bourdieu 1990:70, 86). Habitus is a "property of actors (whether individuals or groups or institutions) that comprises a structured and structuring structure" (Bourdieu 1994:170). Maton (2014) points out that, for Bourdieu (1990:53), "the structure comprises a system of dispositions which generate perceptions, appreciation and practices". Bourdieu (1993:87) suggests that these "dispositions or tendencies are durable in that they last over time, and are transportable in being capable of becoming active within a variety of theatres of social action". Habitus as a complex amalgamation of past and present is "a socialized subjectivity" and "the social embodied" (Bourdieu & Wacquant 1992:127–128). Bourdieu describes the habitus as "durably inculcated by the possibilities and impossibilities, freedoms and necessities, opportunities and prohibitions inscribed on the objective conditions" (1990:54). He points out that habitus consists not only of mental abilities, but also of bodily gestures and comportments that individuals are not aware of. He explains the notion of habitus as a form of embodiment thus:

> It [habitus] is the socialised body. The structured body, a body which has incorporated the immanent structures of a world or of a particular sector of that world – a field – and which structures the perception of that world as well as action in that world. (Bourdieu 1998:81)

This suggests that habitus is created in and through social processes and that the body is central to the emergence and formation of habitus.

Bourdieu (1977:72) sees institutional space as a "strategy-generating principle enabling agents to cope with unforeseen and ever changing situations". Bourdieu and Wacquant (1992:129) suggest that individuals adopt strategies to find a "feel for the game". They define strategies as "objectively orientated lines of action which the social agents continually construct in and through practice" (1992:129). Jenkins (1992:51) explains that, for Bourdieu, strategies are "the on-going result of the interaction between the dispositions of the habitus and the constraints and possibilities which are the reality of any given social field". The relationship between field and habitus is thus fundamental to understanding social practices. For Bourdieu (2000:150–151), the relation between habitus and field can be regarded as "a meeting of two evolving logics and histories". In the evolving higher education space, the habitus of students is constantly emerging and reproducing educational capital and practices.

Bourdieu argues that habitus "realizes itself, becomes active only in the relation to a field, and the same habitus can lead to very different practices and stances depending on the state of the field" (1990:116). Bourdieu uses the analogy of a game to discuss social life and compares the game to the social field. According to Thomson (2014:67), "there is no level playing ground in the social field; players who begin with particular forms of capital are advantaged at the outset because the field depends on, as well as produces, more of that capital". The habitus plays a crucial role in being able to master the game. For Bourdieu:

> Habitus as the feel for the game is the social game embodied and turned into a second nature. Nothing is simultaneously freer and more constrained than the action of the good player. (Bourdieu & Wacquant 1992:63)

Some players are able to understand the rules of the game, use their capital productively, and progress further than others. Bourdieu points out that "when habitus encounters a social world of which it is the product, it is like a 'fish in water': it does not feel the weight of the water, and it takes the world about itself for granted" (Bourdieu & Wacquant 1992:127). Here, one's habitus is in alignment with the field and one is able to play the game successfully. In contrast, the students in this study 'feel the weight of the water' as their habitus is misaligned to the university field. Despite this misalignment, I discuss below how the students were able to construct practices to survive the uneven field of the university.

The discussion below focuses on how the selected students construct their practices by examining how they went about producing their learning dispositions in their interaction with the university field. Wacquant's (2014, 2015) elaboration of the concept of habitus allows me to illustrate in this chapter how students engage in their learning and the learning practices they produce as a core constitutive element of their educational engagement practices. By examining the field, capital and habitus of disadvantaged students, I seek to focus on the forms of capital that students produce in their engagement with the university. Exploring students' educational engagement practices based on a Bourdieusian theoretical framework allows me to examine the motivating factors that shaped their educational experiences and the forms of capital they cultivated at university.

The students' horizontal engagement practices at the university

In this section, I focus on the horizontal engagement practices that students are engaged in at the university. Horizontal engagement practices refer to those practices that students establish that give them the capacity to mediate their educational engagement at the university. I suggest that these types of practices enable students who feel alienated from the university environment to withstand, interpret and adopt strategies that mitigate their initial sense of alienation at the university. The data show that students took it upon themselves to develop such practices, supported by peers and informed by their community cultural wealth (Yosso 2005), in order to find a footing from which to launch themselves into their university education.

Some of the examples of these horizontal engagement practices are students seeking like-minded peers and trusting networks to engage in their studies. The formation of study groups was an important horizontal engagement practice. Thabisa was part of two study groups, one at the residence and one in the department. In the department, she studied with another student from Tshwane who shared the same language and culture. Musa found other students who were studying the same course and who lived in the same area, and formed a study group of three students. The families of the three students supported them by allowing the boys to live and study together at their homes on a rotational basis. The supportive role of the family was crucial in their quest for higher education. Other students, who had similar family and educational background, played a key role in enabling these horizontal practices and assisted students with feeling a sense of belonging at the university which provided them with further motivation to persist in their studies.

My research revealed that students often approached older senior students who were in the same course about their learning. The older students offered advice, guidance and insight into the lecturers' style and approach. Students also approached other peers who were achieving better academic results for help. These knowledgeable peers assisted the students to engage in their work in productive ways. One participant identified that her reading and note-taking skills were ineffective for university study and discussed learning strategies with her peers. Students also studied together informally outside classrooms in order to explain difficult concepts to each other.

The horizontal practices created through their peer support were essential for them to establish a foothold at the university in order to establish a sense of connection needed to engage more deeply in their learning. The data revealed that the peer support strategies adopted by students were characterised by: (1) students seeking like-minded peers and trusting networks to engage in their studies; (2) students forming study groups to engage with the course; (3) students seeking older, more experienced students for advice and guidance about the course content; and (4) students approaching more knowledgeable peers regarding the course.

Through these horizontal practices the students were able to establish strong peer connections and at the same time they were able to engage with the course. These practices, I argue, allowed the selected students to mediate complex academic practices, and in the process they were able to adopt practices to establish their learning at the university. In other words, the acquisition of this mediating capacity addressed their 'fish out of water' experiences which they initially encountered during their studies. Their mediating capacity played a decisive role in their attempts to address the hysteresis between their (pre-university) habitus and the dissonant university field. They had entered the university with constraints associated with their poor schooling such as their inadequate knowledge of school Science and their undeveloped English language skills.

Developing their mediating capacity took place in relation to what they experienced as an uneven and unresponsive university field. In other words, the university failed to understand, connect with and address these students' peculiar requirements for university study, causing their initial sense of distance and alienation from the university field, from their courses of study, the university infrastructure and lecturers.

They responded by finding ways to mitigate the consequences of such alienation. Their strategies allowed them to close the gap between themselves (in particular their pre-university habitus) and the university field. In the absence of systemic support, they worked out how to engage in their learning at the university, how the university functioned in relation to provision of their courses of study, and how its institutional support structures were set up to support their education.

Their mediating capacity was further facilitated by them drawing liberally on the cultural wealth (Yosso 2005) in their families and communities such as emotional support, navigational and survival abilities, and linguistic and aspirational capital in order to develop the capacity to mitigate their 'fish out of water' university experiences. Family capital was central in their educational engagement as students drew on "cultural knowledges nurtured among families that carry a sense of community history, memory and cultural intuition" for their educational engagement (Yosso 2005:79). Parents' moral discourses about education encouraged students to aspire and persist in their studies (Norodien-Fataar 2016). Mothers' emotional support and encouragement were essential and formed the bases from which students could access and engage in their studies at university.

Strengthened by their family capital, at the same time they formed connections with peers from similar backgrounds which provided them with a sense of belonging that mitigated their sense of isolation at university. They nurtured these trusting peer networks early on during their studies as a means of negotiating their university studies. It is thus evident that such active and collaborative engagement with their student peers represented a form of horizontal field-based engagement that enabled them to acquire the capacity to mediate their educational engagement with the university. These horizontal engagement practices were mostly accomplished parallel to the formal educational platform of the university, which failed to connect with their requirements as disadvantaged students. The students took it upon themselves to develop practices, supported by peers and informed by their community cultural wealth, to launch themselves into their university education. This in turn provided them the basis for their immersion in their study programmes.

Establishing intersecting forms of engagements and confronting the university's field

In this section, I focus on the ability of students to accumulate forms of capital necessary to engage in the university field. Accumulating these forms of capital enabled them to engage in the mainstream of the university where they acquired the forms of capital they needed for successful university study. In their attempt to accumulate forms of capital, the students began to shift their parallel engagement practices from the margins to the centre of the university with the constant support and backing of their peers. Engaging with the mainstream structures of the university was crucial in order to deepen their educational engagements and to acquire the social and cultural capital necessary to 'play the game' at the university. While still depending on their student peer support networks, they started to engage with and confront the formal university structures to address the challenges they experienced with, for example, learning to study in English, grappling to understand core concepts, and acquiring the requisite Science-related knowledge in their courses.

Students developed strategies to engage in productive ways with their lecturers to bridge the gap between their parallel learning practices and the formal university knowledge structures. Engaging with lecturers was a key strategy in their attempt to accrue the requisite forms of capital in the field for successful course study. Musa struggled with studying food chemistry and consulted a lecturer about ways in which to approach his studies. The lecturer stressed the importance of spending more time on a subject. Musa reflected that "the more I put time into it [food chemistry], at least I was having a better understanding", while Naledi consulted her lecturer about study techniques for Microbiology and received advice on how to study the subject more effectively. The lecturer emphasised writing short summaries, memorising and identifying key concepts.

Students reported that they often consulted lecturers for their own as well as their study group's benefit. They reported back to their groups any information or skills that lecturers gave them during consultations. The students also referred to lecturers whom they regarded as role models and whom they admired. They were impressed by their dedication and commitment to community-based initiatives and their academic work. They felt that lecturers who reached out and were friendly and welcoming were easier to approach for assistance with the problems that they experienced with their learning.

The students identified that engaging with lecturers after assessments was a useful strategy in order to participate more meaningfully in their learning. They felt that they could identify their strengths and weaknesses during the post-test feedback. Some lecturers assisted the students to make connections with the academic support services such as the teaching and learning unit which allowed students to seek support from academic literacy lecturers and writing consultants. This was particularly useful for students who had to write scientific reports. The lecturers' interaction with students made it possible for students to acquire the capital needed to engage in their education at the university.

One of the significant features of my data was the impact of negative engagements between lecturers and students. Some of the selected students received negative post-test feedback from their lecturers in which they were severely criticised. The students also raised concerns about some of their lecturers' lack of sensitivity to the diverse student needs and referred to the use of unfamiliar languages in the classroom by some lecturers. My data showed that students resisted these negative engagements by confronting lecturers about their behaviour. Yosso (2005:80) refers to this as "resistant capital" which is regarded as the "knowledges and skills fostered through oppositional behaviour that challenges inequality". Resistance and contestation was therefore a feature of educational engagement practices amongst the selected students.

Besides engaging with lecturers, another intersecting practice was the students' ability to engage with information communication technologies (ICTs) to facilitate their educational engagement at university. The use of mobile technologies such as cellphones was key to students' educational engagement and became an essential ICT tool with which to engage in their learning. Podcasts made available by lecturers were regarded as a useful tool with which to engage in the course. The students downloaded the relevant podcast lectures to their cellphones from the university's Blackboard platform and gradually became more skilled at using the computer and social media tools. The podcasts enabled them to listen to the lectures at home for the purpose of which they began to utilise active listening techniques.

The students accessed YouTube lectures in order to understand the concepts that they did not comprehend in the classroom. YouTube videos were used in order to augment the university lectures and to gain a deeper understanding of difficult concepts. YouTube videos were mostly accessed on campus in order to circumvent the high costs of data. The use of mobile technology such as cellphone via WhatsApp was a very popular strategy among students as they could take pictures and send them to each other regarding their academic work when they were not together. The students also discussed group assignments and formed group chats whereby they would clarify concepts by engaging with others on WhatsApp. Mobile technologies and social media tools became an integral part of students' learning experience as they developed various activities to strengthen their learning. Students were able to share, connect, collaborate, create and disseminate knowledge and information via mobile technologies in their attempt to mediate their educational environment. They became skilled at using ICTs and mobile technologies to access social media tools in order to augment their learning and create purposeful activities. ICTs became part of their embodied learning activities and central to the students' educational engagement.

Consulting with lecturers, engaging in assessment feedback, ICT and utilising academic support structures became key intersecting forms of engagement practices for the students to acquire the capital they needed to succeed at the university. I contend that activating and (re)positioning their practices from the periphery to the centre of the university field represents a type of 'transversal engagement' (see Bourdieu 1984) practice. By 'transversal engagement', I refer to empowering practices generated by the students to bridge the gap between their horizontal engagement practices and the academic structures of the university. These intersecting or bridging (transversal) forms of engagement practices established a link between the students and the university's formal educational offerings such as the lectures, the support infrastructure, their department of study and their course lectures. These practices thus enabled them to engage with the structures of the university in meaningful ways. While it was the students' ability to develop their mediating capacity, as outlined in the first dimension, that enabled them to enter and engage with formal university structures, the students were now in a position to confront the university's uneven field conditions by finding ways to engage with the formal structures of the university. Supported by their peers who assisted them in developing a sense of belonging through their horizontal engagement practices, the students developed greater confidence to engage in their university education.

The students' transversal engagement practices were thus practices that involved a crucial shift from their horizontal peer-based support practices to establishing interconnections with the (vertical) formal structures of the university and, as such, signified a qualitative change in their learning practices. Bourdieu (1984:126) suggests that "transverse movement entails a shift from one (part of the) field to another (part of the) field and the reconversion of one type of capital into another ... (which accords with) the vertical dimension". Accordingly, the students' transversal practices enabled them to move from the periphery to the centre of the university field, i.e. the vertical dimension, and represented their ability to change and adapt their practices in order to accumulate the required forms of capital for successful study.

These types of practices allowed the students to confront the university's field conditions and go on to establish their emerging learning dispositions. In other words, instead of establishing their practices parallel to the university's formal structures, as in the case of the previous dimension, the students now accumulated forms of capital within the formal structures of the university.

Building embodied learning practices (habitus) to establish their educational engagement at the university

The students' horizontal engagement practices provided them with the necessary affective connections that enabled them to find their way to the centre of the university field and to accumulate the necessary forms of capital for their educational engagement. The students were now in a position to build embodied learning practices. This is the third dimension of their logic of educational engagement practice. These embodied practices were key to the formation of what I describe as their emergent learning habitus. I offer the concept of learning habitus in reference to the students' ability to acquire the dispositions and capacity to engage in their learning at the university. Central to their learning habitus acquisition was their cultivation of a series of embodied practices that enabled them to engage with their learning in their programmes of study.

The students cultivated their learning practices based on establishing disciplined and strict learning routines. They committed themselves to long hours of study. They established learning activities individually as well as in groups and were constantly involved in various projects to improve their learning effectiveness. The students became focused on developing productive learning activities. In their quest to establish productive activities, they became attentive to the skills and knowledge that they needed to engage successfully in their respective courses.

They focused intently on the intellectual aspects of their learning and displayed a willingness to practice and become competent in acquiring the scientific skills and knowledge offered by their courses. They concentrated on learning practices that supported key scientific tasks such as writing reports and doing experiments which were essential for their course learning. Scientific report writing was a vital skill that they developed during their undergraduate years. They were determined to acquire the knowledge and cognitive ability to engage in the course.

Grappling with scientific concepts in a second language, often by mobilising their mother tongue to develop an understanding of these concepts, was important for mastering the course content. Students explained that they would break concepts or words down and consult dictionaries to be able to understand their meaning. They actively worked to understand the scientific concepts in their courses such as taxonomy, velocity, momentum, microorganism and nomenclature. The students reported that they consulted dictionaries, discussed the meaning of the concepts and used isiXhosa and English interchangeably. They also reported that they developed a playful engagement with the concepts. These linguistic strategies thus enabled them to become affectively connected to their courses which thereby supported them in reinforcing and thickening their learning. The relationship between the affective aspects of their learning and their knowledge acquisition was central to their embodied learning.

The students developed individual academic literacy strategies and chose a specific technique rooted in their personal learning styles. They deliberately applied personal strategies to understand the reading content. Wacquant (2015:3) refers to these types of techniques as the "experience and training" that people undergo in order to develop the necessary skills to survive and thrive in their surroundings. These cognitive practices can be seen as a personal learning strategy which emerges as "embodied practical knowledge" (Wacquant 2015:2). These personal learning strategies enabled the students to find strategies to learn difficult Science content and to persist in their studies. Some of these strategies were writing down and highlighting key words, mind mapping and developing strategies to read academic texts. Their ability to harness their academic literacy skills became a vital part of their embodied learning engagement.

The students developed embodied learning practices which characterised the logic of their educational engagement. These embodied practices were key to the formation of what I describe as their emergent learning habitus. I argue that it was the intersection of the affective, cognitive and conative dimensions of their learning that was thus central in the formation of their learning habitus. In other words, the students' motivation for their studies, the generation of purposeful activities, and their ability to focus on the scientific knowledge of their courses were interrelated aspects of their learning that developed simultaneously to generate a learning habitus for their educational engagement at the university. The development of students' learning habitus was a critical part of their 'logic of educational engagement' and the nature of their educational engagement at university.

Conclusion

In this chapter, I have discussed how the selected first generation disadvantaged students constructed and developed mediation practices for their educational engagement at the university. I argued that the students developed a particular 'logic of educational engagement' practices, namely: (1) the elaboration of a set of horizontal practices on the margins of the university field in order to address their alienation; (2) the establishment of intersecting forms of engagements that confronted the university's field and which enabled them to engage in their learning in the mainstream university field and accrue the required forms of capital needed to engage in their learning; and (3) the building of embodied learning practices that enabled them to develop a learning habitus in order to establish their educational engagement at the university. The logic of their educational engagement was thus built on practices which were characterised by a learning habitus formed at the intersection of the affective, conative and cognitive dimensions of their learning.

References

Bitzer E. 2009. Academic and social integration in three first-year groups: A holistic perspective. *South African Journal of Higher Education*, 23(2):225–245.

Boughey C. 2007. Marrying equity and efficiency: The need for third generation academic development, *Perspectives in Education*, 25(3):27–38.

Bourdieu P & Passeron JC. 1977. *Reproduction in education, society and culture*, R Nice (trans). London: Sage.

Bourdieu P. 1990. *The logic of practice*, R Nice (trans). Cambridge: Polity Press.

Bourdieu P & Wacquant L. 1992. *An invitation to reflexive sociology*. Cambridge: Polity Press.

Bourdieu P. 1994. *Distinction: A social critique of a judgement of taste*: Cambridge: Harvard University Press.

Bourdieu P. 1998. *Practical Reason: On the Theory of Action*. Stanford: Stanford University Press.

Bourdieu P. 2000. *Pascalian meditations*. Cambridge: Polity Press.

Bourdieu P. 2005. *The Social Structures of the Economy*. Cambridge: Polity Press

Bourdieu P. 2006. "The forms of capital". In: H Lauder, P Brown, JA Dillabough & AH Halsey (eds). *Education, globalisation and social change*. Oxford: Oxford University Press. 105–118.

Bozalek V. 2009. "Institutional responses to challenges related to student performance". *Report on the CHEC/PGWC joint regional seminar on student performance*. Sharman Wickham (ed). School of Public Health, University of Western Cape.

Cross M & Atinde V. 2014. The Pedagogy of the marginalised: Understanding how historically disadvantaged students negotiate their epistemic access in a diverse university environment. *The Review of Education, Pedagogy and Cultural Studies*, 37:308–325. https://doi.org/10.1080/10714413.2015.1065617

Jenkins R. 1992. *Pierre Bourdieu*. 2nd Edition. London: Routledge. https://doi.org/10.4324/9780203317471

Kapp R, Badenhorst E, Bangeni B, Craig TS, Janse van Rensburg V, Le Roux K, Prince R, Pym J & Van Pletzen E. 2014. Successful students' negotiation of township schooling in contemporary South Africa. *Perspectives in Education*, 32(3):50–61.

Kuh GD. 2009. What Student Affairs Professionals Need to Know About Student Engagement. *Journal of College Student Development*, 50(60):683–706. https://doi.org/10.1353/csd.0.0099

Lingard B. 2013. *Politics, Policies and Pedagogies in Education. The selected works of Bob Lingard.* London and New York: Routledge.

Makgoba MW. 1997. *Mokoko: the Makgoba affair: a reflection on transformation.* Florida Hills, South Africa: Vivlia.

Marshall D & Case J. 2010. Rethinking 'disadvantage' in higher education: a paradigmatic case study using narrative analysis. *Studies in Higher Education*, 35(5):491–504. https://doi.org/10.1080/03075070903518386

Maton K. 2014. "Habitus". In: M Grenfell (ed). *Pierre Bourdieu Key Concepts.* 2nd Edition. London and New York: Routledge. 48–64.

Mckay J & Devlin M. 2016. "Low income doesn't mean stupid and destined for failure": challenging deficit discourses around students from low SES backgrounds in higher education. *International Journal for Inclusive Education*, 20(4):347–363. https://doi.org/10.1080/13603116.2015.1079273

Moore R. 2014. "Capital". In: M Grenfell (ed). *Pierre Bourdieu Key Concepts.* 2nd Edition. London and New York: Routledge. 48–64.

Smit R. 2012. Towards a clearer understanding of student disadvantage in higher education: problematising deficit thinking. *Higher Education Research & Development*, 31(3):369–380. https://doi.org/10.1080/07294360.2011.634383

Strydom P. 2009. "Student engagement and student success". *Report on the CHEC/PGWC joint regional seminar on student performance.* Sharman Wickham (ed). School of Public Health, University of Western Cape.

Thomson P. 2014. "Field". In: M Grenfell (ed). *Pierre Bourdieu Key Concepts.* 2nd Edition. London and New York: Routledge. 65–80.

Van Schalkwyk S. 2009. "Institutional responses to challenges related to student performance". *Report on the CHEC/PGWC joint regional seminar on student performance.* Sharman Wickham (ed). School of Public Health, University of Western Cape.

Wacquant L. 2014a. Homines in Extremis: What fighting scholars teach us about habitus. *Body & Society*, 20(2):3–17. https://doi.org/10.1177/1357034X13501348

Wacquant L. 2014b. Putting habitus in its place: A rejoinder to the symposium. *Body & Society*, 20(2):118–139. https://doi.org/10.1177/1357034X14530845

Wacquant L. 2015. For a sociology of flesh and blood. *Qualitative Sociology*, 38:1–11. https://doi.org/10.1007/s11133-014-9291-y

Yosso T. 2005. Whose culture has capital? A critical race theory discussion of community cultural wealth. *Race, Ethnicity and Education*, 8(1):69–91. https://doi.org/10.1080/1361332052000341006

Chapter 7

Back from the edge: Exploring adult education and training as second chance opportunity for adult students

Doria Daniels

Introduction

Adult education and training (AET) pathways have been created to facilitate a second educational beginning for adults in South Africa who had no or inadequate access to formal education and training. Initially, these were older adult students, often full-time workers, who were illiterate. Over the last two decades the demographics of AET have radically changed as AET centres are now occupied by a student population of school-going age. This new AET population are young adults who do not have access to the formal school system any more and have been denied re-entry into the formal school system due to a variety of factors such as teenage pregnancy, disciplinary problems, and criminal transgressions. One of the reasons for the high volume of high school age students in AET is the absence or lack of a system or pathway between formal schooling and adult education and training that could cater for those students who fall out of the formal school system. AET therefore becomes their default option when high schools refuse re-admission to these students. In an educational milieu where the school dropout rate is high, the lack of accountability of the state to facilitate these young people's educational re-entry into the formal schooling system necessitates that this issue be brought into sharper focus.

For the purpose of this chapter I favour a social justice orientated theoretical position that links education to political accountability and the state. In South Africa's educational history, the separation of adults' basic education and children's basic education rested upon an understanding that non-formal education should provide educational opportunities to adults who historically did not have access to formal schooling, while the formal school system should provide basic education to children. However, this stance has resulted in the neglect of adult basic education and its subordination to children's schooling as a national educational priority. In the past two decades, there has been an educational climate change, with government placing AET within the General Education and Training (GET) band of formal education (see DoE 2000). The redistributive remedy for adult basic education's marginalisation was to incorporate AET in the National Qualifications Framework (NQF), as a system parallel to basic education for children (DHET 2013). This educational policy facilitated AET's formalisation and created academic continuity for adult students beyond the GET band. The transformation of adult basic education was however conceptualised with the illiterate adult in mind, not the literate adolescent who discontinued his or her formal schooling. Though the education department admitted that there was neglect of adult basic education, the government did not immediately redistribute its educational resources to address AET's challenges. I argue that the AET Directorate in the Department of Education has not taken cognisance of the shift in AET demographics and, in Fraser's (2009) terms, misrecognised how the changed AET demographics have created different challenges within AET.

The educational goals of the current intake of AET students are different from those of the traditional AET student. Whereas the motivation of traditional AET students was to become literate, the current mostly literate AET students are in pursuit of a General Education and Training Certificate (GETC), which will allow re-entry to formal education. This new generation of AET students are young, formally schooled, and often had a troubled (past) relationship with schooling. Some of them could not be promoted beyond Grade 7 and therefore had to leave formal schooling, while others had dropped out of school or were expelled for delinquency and disciplinary reasons. Some committed crimes where court judgements would stipulate that they complete their formal schooling. AETCs are thus compelled to enrol such young people, even when they are as young as 15 years of age, as they are classified as out-of-school youth and now fit the definition of the adult student.

The unwillingness or inability of high schools to admit these students a second time round has caused them to generally distrust educational institutions and their educators. However, AET has a history of working with marginalised adults and seems to be a much more welcoming environment for marginalised, vulnerable students. Many of these new generation AET students, despite their failure at school, go on to perform reasonably well on the GET exit exam, and many end up completing their schooling at the AET centres.

My interest in pursuing the issue of AET student success stems from my involvement in a commissioned national research project on AET institutional efficacy. The national research team of South African academics (Umalusi 2015) studied AET institutional efficacy by exploring their governance, teaching, learning and their institutional relations. As the primary researcher for the Western Cape, I conducted research at three sites: a medium-security prison AETC, a state AETC situated in a township, and a semi-private AETC. At each of these institutions, I interviewed various role players such as students, AET facilitators and administrators. In this chapter, the focus shifts from the institution to the adult student.

This chapter seeks to advance an account of the ways in which three adult students navigate AET in search of a GETC, in order to establish viable productive lives. Part of this account is an exploration of the networks within AET that made it possible for these adults to achieve success. The question that I explore in this chapter is, "How is education mediated by students in these AETCs to facilitate their educational success?" I presume that the stories these students would tell of their individual educational experiences would be co-constructions of their own educational histories, their engagements with the formal educational system, and their conversations with me, the researcher. My contention is that all these influences intersect and shape their thinking and their actions regarding their education, which they are now encountering as adult students.

I find support in Liamputtong and Ezzy's writing (2005:132) that locate narratives "at the intersection of history, biography and society". Narrative inquiry allowed me the opportunity to engage with these adults on a one-to-one basis, and presented me the opportunity to probe into aspects of their lives that could inform my understanding of the chapter's research focus (Mertens 2014; Creswell 2003). Semi-structured personal interviews facilitated the interactional knowledge collected (Terre Blanche, Durrheim & Painter 2006; Patton 2002). For the analysis, I made use of Chase's (2005) five interrelated analytical lenses that look at the narrative as a vehicle for human action, narrator voice, social circumstances as constraints to narrations, social situatedness of the narrative, and the researcher as narrator. The data were analysed with three strategic phases of the individuals' educational lives in mind, namely their childhood educational experiences, their continued education in adulthood and their educational navigations in the AETCs.

This chapter is based on the educational journeys of three adults whom I have given the pseudonyms, Hennie, Karlien and Bronson. Through a wider lens on their pathways, I first consider key aspects of their often difficult and challenging life contexts. I then consider how such contexts position and influence their educational quests. I follow this with an exploration of aspects of their childhood educational experiences, as well as the AETC as a dynamic educational space that harnessed 'triggers' which allowed them to generate productive educational paths. I argue that these triggers, together with the self-efficacy of the adult students, help position them in ways that facilitate success. What the chapter thus does is bring into critical focus the role that their childhood contexts and histories played in their negative experiences with formal schooling. The final section of the chapter explores how the AETCs served to restore trust in their capabilities and advance self-efficacy which, in effect, placed them as adults on a road of possibility. The chapter combines aspects of Bourdieu (1977) and Yosso's (2005) theoretical resources to advance a theoretical framework to inform my analysis of these disenfranchised adults' educational journeys in respect of their childhood contexts, schooling experiences and their educational success at the AECTs.

Theoretical framework

The chapter firstly draws on Bourdieu's analytical tools of field, habitus and capital to explain how the participants in the study navigate their world. Thereafter, I introduce Yosso's (2005) community cultural wealth theory as a second analytical tool to understand adults' second chance success in education. I start with Bourdieu's concept of field (Bourdieu & Wacquant 1992:97) which refers to "a network of objective historical relations between positions". The 'field' explored in this chapter is the combined educational landscape that the adult students traversed, which includes their formal schooling, the AET context and programme, facilitators and support services. Bourdieu used the analogy of a game with rules and positions to explain his concept of field. Similar to how rules and regulations guide the game and define positions, so too, the social spaces that the students inhabit are guided by the rules of engagement and the roles that they and others in it, take on. The field is, however, a dynamic space in which there is constant vying for prime positioning and power. Moreover, all actors have a relationship with the outcome of the action; thus, the actions they take facilitate a particular outcome. To explain the repeated patterns of such daily actions, Bourdieu (2006) introduced the term 'habitus', which refers to an individual's internalised ways of doing and being.

Bourdieu (1998:11) further describes a 'field' as social space that is "an invisible reality that cannot be shown but which organizes agents' practice and representations". It is through this tacit understanding of the field that one comes to understand social practices and how these practices are facilitated. Fataar (2008) further states that by studying the social spaces (fields) that people occupy, one can develop an understanding of what people become when they inhabit these spaces, as well as how individuals use social spaces and what they produce out of such spaces. The point that both Fataar (2008) and Bourdieu (1998) make is that people's perceptions, knowledge and understandings are fashioned and moulded by the social and cultural environments that they reside in. Importantly, it gives one insight into what people identify as the resources or the capital that they use to navigate their worlds successfully. 'Field' is useful in advancing insight into what resources were available in the social spaces that the three adult students in this study navigated as children growing up in difficult circumstances, and the types of capital that they acquired to become successful in AET. By analysing the students' social spaces, one can unmask how advantage and disadvantage play out in their lives, and how these influenced their decisions and stance on education later in life.

Bourdieu's thinking about power in society is captured by his concept of cultural capital. He argues that in a class-defined society social spaces are set up in particular ways so that some groups are seen to belong and others not, depending on the value of the cultural and social capital that they have accumulated. Bourdieu's term, 'cultural capital' refers to the accrued cultural knowledge, skills and abilities that privileged groups in society possess. For example, the middle-class family accumulates knowledge about money and assets, which is then the economic or material capital that enhances their and their children's position in the social hierarchy. Parents know that their distribution of cultural values and class-based practices to their children will equip them to compete for positions of power in society and help them to maintain it. Bourdieu (in Bourdieu & Passeron 1977) identifies social class as determinant of whether a group's knowledge is valued by the broader society. In a study of an American worker-class context (Johnson 2015:31) reference is made to the 'hidden injury' sustained by families when their lack of economic and cultural capital prevents them from purchasing the best education for their children, and how they then experience the symbolic violence directed at them by society. In a hierarchical society the production and exchange of knowledge is often racially defined and class stratified. Bourdieu (1977) uses the word 'doxa' to refer to the 'taken-for-granted' knowledge that society has about certain groups. These are opinions and views about their abilities, how they talk, how they interact, their patterns of behaviour and even their value systems. Bourdieu (2000) describes these doxic influences as subconsciously conditioning people in how they think about themselves in relation to others in society, and their preconceived ideas of the roles that they can and should perform in society.

Through this lens working-class students might internalise the societal limitations placed on their competencies as normal for their group and may find the misrecognition of their potential acceptable due to their perceptions of their limited worth and capability when compared to middle-class students. Weininger and Lareau's (2003) research found that middle-class-associated advantage is constructed and maintained through actual and virtual capital that is accrued through connections and durable networks with significant others. This type of capital Bourdieu (1977) defines as social capital. Rocco and Suhrcke (2012) describe social capital as a valuable social resource with a variety of dimensions that has the capability of improving individuals' social and emotional wellbeing. It is a system or network of elaborate interactions that individuals identify and access to facilitate success. Social capital can also be an exchange of resources within and beyond the complex networks or systems (Lareau & Weininger 2003). Operating as networks, they regulate the efficient flow of information for the benefit of those within the relationship network. Schools, as microcosms of society, adopt the values of the dominant class in society, which is the middle class. Access to, and familiarity with, such networks positively influence the life chances of students from middle-class backgrounds and differentially aid their adjustment to school, and later, society (Lareau & Weininger 2003).

For my research among vulnerable and poor individuals I found the community cultural wealth (CCW) theory of Yosso (2005) a more suitable framework for analysing the adult students' narratives. This framework acknowledges the mutual engagement and influences between individuals and the communities they grew up in. Yosso's CCW theory extends and provides a different reading of Bourdieu's perspective of cultural and social capital. Yosso explains how schools use a specific form of knowledge as the norm, which positions all other forms of knowledge as subordinate. Thus, when poor students access schools with cultural capital that the school does not recognise as the norm, these students struggle to navigate the school environment successfully. This happens when the school (as social space) engages with the students' cultural capital as if it is deficient, and hence of lesser value. The participation of such students in this space is thus defined by a reduced mode of being. By centring the middle class in his theory, Bourdieu does not theorise the capital that working-class communities produce in their struggles "to survive and resist macro and micro forms of oppression" (Yosso 2005:77). For Yosso, the cultural wealth that exists in working-class communities is represented by "an array of knowledge, skills, abilities and contacts" (2005:77) that they possess and use to survive under often harsh circumstances.

Yosso (2005) states that racial and class marginalised communities nurture cultural wealth through six forms of capital that she introduces as aspirational, navigational, social, linguistic, familial and resistant capital. These are however not stand-alone forms of capital; rather they are dynamic inter-related practices that build on one another. I contend that cultural and social capital are constantly being re-negotiated, adjusted and produced when individuals move between real and virtual spaces on their life journeys. Rose, Clear, Waring and Scully (2000) differentiate between the structural and individual level effects of social capital, pointing out that the two involve different processes of social capital. The distinction between the structural and individual level effects of social capital is important in my analysis of, for example, Bronson who accesses his AET in the context of his incarceration in prison. In a strictly regimented space such as a prison, the typical pathways for accessing social capital might not be available. Moreover, incentives for developing social capital in prison may be different from the social capital drivers within the community. For example, when the inmate is confined to a cell with just one other inmate, his opportunities to network with others are taken away. Furthermore, access to systems that could benefit the individual's accumulation of cultural and social capital are prioritised differently in a prison setting, as access is subject to the regulations of the prison authorities. In the literature, collective efficacy and social capital are used interchangeably, as if they are similar qualities. Sampson, Raudenbush and Earls (1997) describe collective efficacy as the process of activating social ties, which is different from social capital, which is the capacity for action that the personal and institutional networks provide (Rose *et al* 2000).

The section above introduced the chapter's theoretical framework, which is used as my conceptual lens in the analysis of the three adults' stories of educational navigation through childhood, schooling and eventually, access and success via their AET pathways. The next section introduces their childhood navigations.

Navigating education through troubled childhoods

This section focuses on Hennie, Bronson and Karlien's induction into, and experiences of formal schooling. They found the school to be an inequitable space that failed to recognise the connections between their poverty-stricken homes and their poor schooling performance. They experienced the rules of engagement in formal schooling as the same for all students, even when the playing fields were not equal. Their teachers held the same expectations of them as students, even when they knew that Hennie, Bronson, Karlien and other students came from challenging home backgrounds that made them vulnerable to early school dropout. In a Bourdieusian (1977) understanding of field, the assumption is that a particular outcome is the result of an action that was taken. Along this line of thinking a student's poor academic performance on tests and exams is the result of poor test or examination preparation or can be used as evidence of the student's lack of intellectual ability to perform optimally. This way of reasoning encourages a deficit placing of that student, and positions the context and circumstances as static environments without agency or influence on the individual's positioning. This line of reasoning misrecognises the structural violence of poverty and how the lack of resources in poor students' homes could be contributing factors in their engagement with schooling. When schools fail to respond to their needs in equitable ways, economically vulnerable students end up marginalised and later, disillusioned with education. Schools are seldom social spaces that are set up to engage with alternative forms of competencies that the students might have. It is thus not surprising that such students internalise a belief that they are incapable of academic success.

Parents are key resources in helping primary school students achieve success in school. However, many students grow up in families where educational support is non-existent because the family's daily life is a constant struggle for survival. Some grow up in contexts where there is no adult supervision in the home because parents are locked away in jail or are too drunk to take responsibility for their children. This was also the case for the three adults in my study. Their homes were characterised by a single or absent parent. Bronson never knew his parents. His grandmother raised him. Karlien and Hennie both lost their fathers at the age of two. Hennie's father committed suicide whilst in jail, and Karlien's father was murdered. Karlien's family disintegrated when her mother "took to the bottle and developed a drinking problem" (Karlien interview 2016). Karlien and her siblings grew up in various foster homes. Bronson's grandmother raised him until she passed away when he was eight years old, after which he was raised by an aunt. These are examples of the structural violence that are inherent in working-class students' contingent social circumstances, but which are largely invisible in the educational discourse on student success.

A thread that runs through all three stories is the role of poverty as a crucial factor in the students' educational failure. As seasonal farm workers, Hennie's parents migrated from farm to farm in search of work opportunities. When the working season ended, the family would have no income or accommodation until they could secure work opportunities in the next seasonal cycle. The continuation of Hennie and his siblings' schooling depended on where the parents were able to find accommodation and work. During these times, when the parents struggled for economic survival, they could not afford to send their children to school. As itinerant migrants, they did not have a community that could tide the family over in times of challenge. The lack of economic capital in their communities meant that financial support structures were limited or non-existent.

Karlien and her siblings were placed in foster care when her single-parent household collapsed. As a ward of the state, this had a devastating effect on her schooling. Every time she was placed with a new family, she had to change schools. Karlien had to repeat three of her grades and was fifteen when she eventually completed primary school. She explained how the foster parents were more interested in the foster grant than in investing in their ward's education. Karlien described her experience as follows:

> My sisters and I ... there was a lot of abuse ... you know, they get the grant for us, but we never have money ... I never had money ... never for school things.
> (Karlien interview 2016)

What comes to mind about Hennie and Karlien's accounts is what Yosso (2005:77) refers to as the "struggles to survive and resist macro and micro forms of oppression".

The migrant lifestyle of both Hennie's family and Karlien's fostering situation placed them at a disadvantage from the beginning of their school life. Their continuous migration or placement in a new foster home were forms of oppression at macro level as it destabilised their basic educational trajectory. Every time they moved it interrupted their schooling and forced them to start over. These created additional layers of subordination for them as students functioning in their class-defined world. When using Bourdieu's (1977) theory as a framework to explain societal and class inequality, one could argue that their family set-up was not conducive for accumulating cultural and social capital. Hennie's parents were uneducated blue-collar workers who were struggling to survive financially. As migrants, they did not stay in a community long enough to establish networks from which to benefit as a family. They did not have a stable income, ideal work conditions or permanent housing. An assumption could be that in his family the potential for cultural capital to be accumulated was limited and what capital was accumulated was of no or limited value in helping Hennie to advance in society.

However, when one explores his narrative through Yosso's (2005) CCW lens, then there is evidence of the ways in which Hennie resisted and survived the various forms of oppression in his life. Hennie knew that if he did well in school he could win academic awards and certificates. Using this as a form of cultural capital, he could turn it into navigational capital for accessing environments not usually available to him. These certificates and awards were forms of cultural capital that had bargaining power beyond his particular primary school context. Twice a year, the top achievers at his school were invited to a school camp at an affluent white school in the town. The invitations to these school camps were privileges that very few students at his small township school enjoyed and were opportunities to access networks reserved for the middle-class student. Hennie's story about the holiday camp is an example of what Yosso (2005) describes as navigational capital, which refers to the skills of manoeuvring through an institution that was not created with a working-class student in mind. The story that Hennie tells, is also an example of a counter-narrative that could be juxtaposed against the stories of the struggling student from a migrant home. In Hennie's case, his story illustrates how migrant family contexts also produce aspiring students who win awards and certificates, and succeed despite their circumstances.

The ways in which parents navigate their disorganised communities vary as is illustrated by my data. In many Western Cape township communities, parents fear that their children, especially their boys, will succumb to the influences of gangsterism. Bronson's grandmother mediated his removal from the community by enrolling him as a boarder at a former Model C school in Franschhoek. In this affluent Boland town he was far away from his community's influences and an inductee to an upper-middle-class culture. This then became the norm against which he measured the township school culture that he had to return to when his grandmother died. He describes the transition from the former Model C school to a township school as follows:

> ... the environment (at the Model C school) was open, free, and friendly ... and now I was sent back to a community that I did not know much about.
> (Bronson interview 2016)

What I read into both Hennie and Bronson's experiences in a middle-class culture at primary school level, was that it mentally set them apart from their peers in the township. Bronson had internalised that the two worlds were different and that the bad things that he was exposed to in the township school "did not happen at my Model C school". Hennie had exposure to, and experience of how social networks or resources can enhance one's life chances. The lesson learnt by Hennie was that in middle-class communities education is valued for the dividends that it pays later on in life. When the students brought this Model C school acquired knowledge into their township school contexts, they internalised that it is a better form of knowledge that is used to subordinate all other forms of knowledge (Yosso 2005). However, these experiences, I argue, also influenced them to respond negatively towards high school education in their townships. Bronson struggled to adapt to his township school. He recalled not fitting in due to his township peers "seeing me as one of those glam[orous] people with those better education because I was at a Model C school".

High school was not a welcoming space for either Bronson or Hennie. Both were new at their schools. Both Hennie and Bronson's poor academic performance marginalised them and contributed to their isolation. In adolescence popularity and peer acceptance are very important. They were in a vulnerable phase of their life course when boys need strong male role models to help guide them to adulthood. It is my contention that Bronson was seeking guidance on how to navigate his world. It is ironic that he would criticise the disorganisation in his township school and its lack of discipline but then rebel against the rules and regulations that his family had imposed on him. When he failed Grade 11, he dropped out of school and moved out of his family's house. Hennie describes his experiences of high school as disempowering. He failed his first year at high school and received a condoned pass at the end of the year. When the process repeated itself in Grade 9, he transferred to a different high school. Hennie eventually dropped out of school in Grade 10.

After they left school, both Hennie and Bronson succumbed to gangsterism. The gangster lifestyle might have provided the structure they sought growing up in disorganised homes without fathers and in communities that provided minimal protection to vulnerable boys against gangsterism. In an alienating world marginalised young males like Hennie and Bronson are perfect recruits for street gangs. Though at the time it provided them with a safe space, this is also where they were introduced to a world of crime and the accumulation of money by illicit means. Hennie's initiation into criminality was gradual. Though he had his first brush with the law as an 11-year-old, it was only after he spent time in jail that he became a full-time gangster. His greatest goal in life then was to move up the number gang rank to become a Number 26[1] gangster. Two years after leaving school, Bronson and four other individuals committed a serious crime for which he was sentenced to 35 years in prison. When I conducted the interview, Bronson was 30 years old.

In this section, I have attempted to show how what happens in childhood homes impacts on the experiences that working-class students have in school. In all three participants' childhoods the connection between their families' social circumstances and their disempowering schooling outcomes were clear. Their families' socio-economic challenges hampered their parents' investment in their children's education in the ways that the school valued. Their educational vulnerabilities stayed unrecognised because the education system engaged with students as if they are all the same; thus those who needed support did not receive any to scaffold their experiences with education. Education then led to the dispositional challenges that they brought into the AET context.

Finding their way back to education

This section starts with an analysis of the incidents in their lives that brought education back into their lives. Hennie recalled how in 2011, at the age of eighteen, while he was out on bail, a friend told him about adult education classes. It brought back happy memories of primary school when he earned diplomas for academic achievement. He attended the information session at the local AETC, but never started classes that year, as "it did not fit my life then". 2011 stood out as the year in which he became a member of the Number 26 gang and the year in which his stepfather died unexpectedly. This gave rise to a series of events that brought him to a crossroads, or what Mezirow (2000) would define as a disconcerting dilemma that resulted in a transformational learning episode. As a hardened criminal caught up in a destructive lifestyle, Hennie could not openly mourn his stepfather's death. Therefore, Hennie spent his days getting high on methamphetamine in an attempt to block out the nightly vigils and praying at his

---

1   The numbers gang has its origins in South African prisons with members and networks on the inside and outside of prison. It consists of the 26, 27 and 28 sub-gang groupings. Hennie fell in with the 26 number. A Number 26 gangster is involved in robberies, smuggling and other monetary related crimes. They are known for their ability to beat the system. During incarceration they are responsible for acquiring drugs, cigarettes and even money.

family home. On one of those nights he collapsed and suffered a breakdown. Hennie described the period from 2011 onward as a period when "a thousand things happened to me". Enrolling at an AETC was one of them.

The shelter for homeless men where Hennie initially lived was a valuable social resource that improved his social and emotional wellbeing. This space presented him with many dimensions of social capital such as safety, trust, formal networks and informal networks (Putnam 2000). For the parolee, it provided a home and safety. It also gave him access to a formal network that directly linked him to the local AETC, as a condition for staying at the shelter was that he should enrol for AET classes. There were also informal networks present at the shelter that connected to the AET, such as other men who were studying towards the GETC, as well as moral support from the shelter's care workers. One of the men that he befriended was Karel who was the top achiever in the country on the AET Level 4 national exams that year and who won the Department of Basic Education's AET student of the year award. Karel's accomplishments received local and national media coverage and were celebrated by his church. Karel's accomplishments inspired Hennie and the support and networks present at the shelter were triggers for Hennie to develop the inner drive and self-motivation to make something of his life.

Karlien's road back to education happened 20 years after she completed primary school. One of her three sons was on the road to delinquency. He was smoking, drinking and getting into trouble at school. When he refused to continue with his schooling one of his high school teachers suggested that Karlien consider the full day AETC in her community as an alternative to him attending school. At the AETC she observed that some of the students were people of her age group, and this in turn awakened her long-time dream of wanting to become a social worker. Karlien and her son both wrote the placement test. Karlien, who had never been to high school, was placed at AET Level 4 while her Grade 9 son was placed at AET Level 3. Karlien's narrative shows that she was at a stage in her life when her family life was in disarray; she was unemployed and her husband had lost his job and was living in a different province trying to secure employment. The family had lost their home and were temporarily living apart from each other. Karlien and her youngest son were living with strangers and the other sons were living with relatives. According to Moerbeeck and Flap (2008), social capital may provide networks that can help adults secure employment. All her life Karlien fancied herself becoming a social worker even though she had only completed primary school. As a social network within the formal structure of education, the AETC was a space where she could accumulate social capital, and hopefully employment. An AET Level 4 pass would give her the equivalency of a Grade 9 qualification which, in turn, would make her eligible to enrol at a Further Education and Training (FET) college where she could study towards a diploma course. In her situation social capital operated to provide greater 'resources' amongst social networks, and thus was expected to contribute towards a better quality of life for her and her family. I am therefore arguing that agency within the individual is a requirement for cultural and social capital to be accrued and then spent. According to Ling and Dale (2014), agency is only viable if individuals believe that they have the capability to do things differently and go about working to establish new life trajectories. When Karlien's assessment score placed her at a higher competency level than her son, it instilled in her the confidence to enrol for AET. Each test that she wrote, and on which she performed well, were opportunities to accrue the motivation she needed to accomplish her goal of becoming a social worker. It strengthened her resolve to gain an education and to identify the networks that she could access through the AETC. These, for me, are examples of aspirational and navigational capital that were being facilitated by Karlien's access to social networks within the AETC. I elaborate on this later in the chapter.

Within Bronson's AET context the existence of social capital and its accumulation was much more complex because it happened during his incarceration. Bronson had no say in whether he wanted to be part of an AET programme. Since 2013, the Department of Correctional Services (DCS) mandated that prisoners who did not have a GETC, have to enrol for AET classes (DCS 2005). I found that the availability of an AETC and its promise of life opportunities did not automatically lead to the participation of inmates in AET. This was because low levels of trust existed between inmates and prison staff which served as a barrier to the construction of social capital (Harvey 2012). Furthermore, the AETC's location within the prison came with restrictions which contributed to inmates' resistance to engage with the social resources that the DCS provided. I understood from Bronson's narrative that inmates opted to participate in AET programmes because of their need for company, not primarily because of a need for educational advancement. He explained that he was trying to access the informal networks in the prison through the AET programme. As social beings humans constantly seek out other humans for company. By participating in the AET programme, the inmates could have contact with other inmates during the day. Contact and communication were beneficial to Bronson's mental wellbeing and survival whilst incarcerated as he was a long-time prisoner. The AET classes presented Bronson with opportunities to escape his isolation and to break the monotony of prison life.

Lafferty, Treloar, Butler, Guthrie and Chambers (2016) explain that outside informal networks of support to inmates are very different from that on the inside, and serve a very different purpose in the prisoner's life. Bronson's family broke off all contact with him when he went to jail. His connections with formal networks outside of prison also stopped when he started his incarceration. The AETC was a social network through which he could accrue an education that would provide him with the type of capital that his family would value. His decision to participate in education was to establish credibility and show his family that he was turning his life around and was investing in his future through becoming educated. His narrative contains examples of how he established formal and informal networks within the prison as well as of how he re-established his informal social network outside of the prison. He suggested that by participating in the AET classes this would allow him,

> ... to regain my family's trust in me ... In prison, one needs your family, their visits. You have to win their trust as no-one trusts you anymore. Thus, in my first year that was my intention, to push time and to please people.
> (Bronson interview 2016)

The three interviewees' re-entry into education was complex because their opportunities to accrue cultural and social capital were restricted by the social and class boundaries of society. Their narratives show that the opportunities to engage with AET were facilitated by their agency to take the initiative, as well as by a social space where formal and informal networks would facilitate educational outcomes. The three stories show that the acquisition of social capital involves mobilising resources among social networks, which, in turn, enables them to develop viable educational pathways.

The AETC context

The three interviewees participated in AET contexts that were very different from each other. Bronson's centre was one of only twelve prison-based AETCs in South Africa. Hennie's AETC was semi-private and located on a university campus, whilst Karlien's AETC was located in an urban township. Bronson described himself as unhappy and lacking confidence when he started attending AET classes. In prison it was mandatory for all inmates without a GETC to enrol in AET. He had been in jail since the age of 17, which was 14 years earlier, and was serving out a 35-year sentence for a serious crime. Though Karlien completed primary school, she repeated three of her grades, and was a lot older than her peers were when she completed her primary schooling. She took 20 years to go back to education. Hennie failed every grade in the three years he attended high school. He was homeless and out on parole when he enrolled for AET. The condition to stay at the shelter was that he participate in AET. They all thus started their AET journeys with many uncertainties. AETCs are replete with life stories like theirs where students enter the educational space with very low self-esteem and distrust and anger toward the educational system. Solórzano and Yosso (2002) refer to these as oppositional behaviours with self-defeating and conformist qualities that could feed back into the system of subordination. However, from my observations, the interviewees' AETCs were prepared for the oppositional behaviours that students brought with them into their institutions. I found that the AETCs had mechanisms in place that allowed for the oppositional behaviour of students to transition into transformative forms of resistance (Solórzano & Yosso 2002). For example, during the intake interview the incoming students are counselled on their strengths and weaknesses and not just their educational competencies. The message that the new enrolees receive is that the AETC is an educational space where adult students receive emotional as well as academic guidance and support. A nurturing disposition seems to be part of the educational philosophy of these AETCs. One of the AETC managers summed it up as follows: "We try to get the adults out as better human beings, not just with a GETC credential." According to her, respect is a value that her AETC identified as an important part of their students' education. They try to model to adult students how respect is lived between student and educator. Furthermore, they use age-appropriate communicative strategies when they engage with students. As one facilitator remarked, the quickest way of getting adult students to rebel, is to treat them like children. What these AETCs had in common were networks of people who served as social resources for aiding students in navigating and achieving educational success. The narratives identify AET facilitators as an important conduit for students' progress. Karlien described them as enablers of her academic success. According to her:

> You can go back 10 or 20 times to ask them to explain to you. ... and if you still do not understand, they will make time during their lunch break for you, and tell you to come. Or they will be available after school, irrespective of what your reason to see them. This is why I persevere ... it is because of the support that the educators give. (Karlien interview 2016)

Bronson was still an adolescent when he committed the crime that led to his incarceration. What access to the AET facilitator as resource did for Bronson was to provide him with an adult role model who could assist with his accumulation of cultural capital. His narrative focuses on the relationships that were established between him and the manager and the educators, not on his successes in the classroom. In his first year in AET, he experienced a lot of support from the centre manager and his educators, and attributed his positive mind-set and his actions to their encouragement and motivation. Bronson talks about how participation in education was a journey of discovering who he is. He reflected on how he has changed in his positioning towards the world, as follows:

> I think back to that first year, and then I compare it to where I am now. I can communicate with people. My family now know that I am taking responsibility for what I did. I can now become a provider in the future and play a role in the community. (Bronson interview 2016)

Their AET environments capacitated students such as Bronson with the linguistic resources to negotiate their reputational positions. Hennie and Bronson were literate and came into AET with formal school credentials and knowledge of how the school system works, which are accumulated cultural and social capital that other AET students might lack. They were confident that their educational history would give them an advantage over the traditional AET student. Bronson did not expect to test at AET Level 2, which was seven grades below the grade he passed, and Hennie at AET Level 4, which was three levels below his high school grade. The two male students rebelled against the outcome, were resentful towards the facilitators and questioned their placement decisions. In Hennie's case, the situation became explosive when he found out that he did not have to attend Level 4 classes as he was already issued with an examination number to write the matric (Grade 12) examinations. He was angry and confronted the centre administrator whom he blamed for the miscommunication. She defused what was an explosive situation by using effective communication to explain the reason for insisting that he complete AET Level 4 first before writing the matric examinations. Hennie lacked experience with the senior phase of high school which the educator identified as a barrier to his future educational success. Her decision was based on her wanting him to improve his chances of passing his matric subjects. Her respectful but firm way of engaging with this adult student made him accept her decision. What started out as oppositional behaviour and resistance became a transformative learning experience for both Hennie and Bronson. Both were encouraged to engage with AET Level 4 as a refresher year in which they would reconnect with schooling to make the transition to further education and training easier.

This incident later became an example of aspirational capital and strengthened Hennie's resolve to achieve educational success. He went on to write the GETC exams to prove to the manager that he was a competent and capable student. He achieved A symbols in three subjects and was the best Western Cape student in Life Orientation. Hennie enrolled for and prepared for the Grade 12 examinations in that same year. This example provides insight into how an enabling social space can capacitate students with resistant capital as well as reverse the negative experiences that they had with formal schooling.

An important form of navigational capital for the students were the links that the AETCs established with outside institutions. By navigational capital I refer to the acquiring of skills and abilities to navigate their way through the AETC and beyond. At Hennie's AETC there were formal links with computer classes, baking courses, learner-driver preparation classes and jewellery making. In Karlien's AETC, skills training courses and apprenticeships were available for students who had completed their GETC. At Brandon's AETC, study through correspondence was facilitated through specially assigned AETC facilitators. At all three AET centres networks were in place that facilitated the students' success beyond the GETC. For example, during the course of the year the managers would arrange career information sessions where FET colleges could address students and advise them on programmes and bursaries that they qualified for, as well as the application processes. What these information sessions accomplished was to strengthen students' aspirational capital as well as expand their navigational capital. When Karlien received her first AET report and saw that she scored a five (on a 1–7 point scale) for Mathematics and seven for all her other subjects, she started believing that "I can become what I want to become. It restored my confidence in my abilities".

The messages that Bronson, Hennie and Karlien received in their AETC environments affirmed their potential to become accomplished and be successful in their education and in life. What comes through in their narratives is how trust gave them confidence in their ability to succeed. The AETCs facilitated their navigation of complementary sites by linking them to FET colleges and skills training programmes. It introduced them to opportunities and opened up new possibilities for them as adults who thought that educational success was not meant for people like them.

Education as aspirational capital to dream about a different future

When Yosso (2005) speaks about aspirational capital she refers to the hopes and dreams that Karlien, Hennie and Bronson have for successful lives and how these fuel their commitment to strive for their educational success. Karlien's narrative elaborates this point. Her childhood dream was to become a social worker even though she knew that it was not possible with a primary school education. Despite repeating three of her grades in primary school and only finishing primary school at the age of fifteen, Karlien still had high educational aspirations for herself. That dream was rekindled when she enrolled for Level 4 at the AET centre. In her year as an AET student, Karlien's results were excellent in all the AET learning areas. When Karlien realised that her dream of becoming a social worker might be unrealistic with just a GETC, she shifted gears and started exploring alternative careers. She could do so because she now had the knowledge or cultural capital that could facilitate her success. She also became knowledgeable about the social networks that she needed to tap into to turn her dreams into reality. Thus, instead of giving up on her dreams, Karlien became committed to explore alternative options available to her once she completes the GETC.

> Yesterday the people from Northlink College were here, and now I have new hope to study administration and then start working at a hospital. Maybe I can do administration work in a hospital. (Karlien interview 2016)

With a GETC she can apply for access to some FET college courses. One of them was the diploma in administrative work. However, should she not gain entry, she would be able to continue with her studies at the AETC and enrol for matric classes instead. Her hopes for the future have shifted beyond merely dreaming about it, to taking the steps to actualise this vision. From her narrative it is clear that she was critically engaging with what the entry-level requirements for diploma studies were and what her investments would have to be to make it a reality. She also thought about a backup plan should the first option not be realised. The aspirational capital she accumulated was intertwined with familial capital which Yosso (2005) refers to as the social and personal human resources that working-class individuals have in their communities. The familial and community networks that these individuals have access to through AET turned their experiences in AET into empowering life experiences.

When Karlien started with Level 4 her home circumstances were very difficult and on quite a few occasions she thought of giving up her studies. Karlien's husband, who had a high school diploma, initially was critical of the quality of her schoolwork. However, when she started doing well on tests he would tell her how proud he was of her. At the time of the interviews, Karlien's family situation was very difficult. Her husband had lost his job and the family had lost their home. She confessed that when she wanted to quit her studies, her mother and sister would talk her out of it and encourage her to persist.

> My sister and mother ... they are very proud of me. They always pushed me, especially with the challenges that I am facing now. They always said I would make it. It is with God's help and my family's help that I am succeeding.
>
> (Karlien interview 2016)

Life is tough for adults like Karlien and Hennie. Both their families live under difficult circumstances which make participation in AET a major sacrifice for both. They are always questioning whether their decision to study is the right one. Hennie lives with his family in a wooden bungalow in someone's backyard. He almost never sees his children as he works seven days a week from 08h00 until 17h00 at a carwash business. On Monday and Thursday evenings he attends classes from 19h30 until 21h30. He worries that he is a bad father to his children, as "school is taking me away from work opportunities". His wife is pregnant and not earning an income, thus the family is surviving on his monthly income of R1 500. During the interview, Hennie looked at me and then said, "You must be thinking, 'Man, you are unwise! Go out and get a better paying job to support your growing family" (Hennie interview 2016).

However, Hennie has big dreams for his future. Though he had just completed AET Level 4, he was already preparing for the high school certificate examination a few months later. He had a future mapped out already. He was working very hard to get good grades in the matric examination as he believed that his investment in his schooling would deliver dividends in the form of a bursary for further study at a university. He was an aspiring university student and dreamt of studying towards a degree in languages. As a future pastor in the church he will need to be eloquent, and "have more impact when speaking, more power" (Hennie interview 2016). This aspiration capital allows adult students like Karlien and Hennie to persevere.

The 30-year-old Bronson's circumstances differ from the other two as he has more than 20 years of a 35-year sentence to serve out in jail. He was seventeen when he was incarcerated and will be 51 years old if he serves out the full sentence. He has already spent nearly half of his life in jail. His dreams of a future are situated in his personal development. The goals and aspirations that he has are more focussed on improving himself as individual. Bronson spoke about how his educators, by talking about their own children and families, provided him with a glimpse into his potential future. Through developing a trusting relationship with his educators they became the stand-in family who believed in him and made him have faith in his potential to succeed in life. Whilst he initially participated in AET to break the monotony of cell life and pass the time, his motivation to participate in education became intrinsic when he started participating in AET to capacitate himself. In my interview with him Bronson talked about "tasting educational success when he did well in exams and passed". I argue that this educational success in AET challenged Bronson's view of himself as worthless and a failure, and led to a paradigm shift about his potentiality as a human being. Educational success became the catalyst for thinking about his future, and his potential to be successful in other spheres of his life too.

> During my stay in prison, I have come to realise that education does not just play a role in what you learn, but also in the person that you become. That has been the catalyst for me to persevere. Now I can communicate with people on a higher level than before. (Bronson interview 2016)

The narrations that I shared and discussed have used Yosso's (2005) aspirational and navigational capital as lens to explain how Karlien and Hennie navigated the AET social space. Both Hennie and Karlien had their own families and tied educational success to better futures for their families. They accrued inspirational and familial capital from family and friends as well as within their educational contexts which were empowering and supportive. Bronson's context and circumstances were different to theirs and his incarceration positioned him differently. He was not privy to outside informal support networks and was entirely dependent on the informal and formal networks within the prison. The navigational capital he acquired was initially externally motivated by the need to establish informal networks to counter his monotonous lifestyle and isolation.

However, once he started engaging with education at the AETC he began to open up a productive educational and life path. This allowed him to become critically reflective of who he is in the world and what his potentialities are for living in that world.

Conclusion

In this chapter, I engaged with adult education and training as a second chance opportunity for adult students who did not complete their basic education. I sought to develop an explanation of the ways in which three adult students navigated AET in search of a GETC in order to establish viable productive lives. Part of this account is an exploration of the networks within AET that made it possible for these adults to achieve educational success. My exploration of their educational success was advanced within an understanding that success is a mediated process influenced by societal position and networks. I explored the nature of the adult students' educational practices within the field conditions of both formal schooling and later adult education and training. My findings show that the socio-economic circumstances and migration patterns of the participants' childhood home contexts served as debilitating factors in their experiences of education. Their struggles in school were not always the result of them being incapable and not investing in their education; rather it was that their families' socio-economic circumstances and their social class placed barriers in their way. The situational challenges of unemployment and poverty threatened their families' stability and forced the families to constantly uproot their children's education. Cultural and social capital accumulation under such circumstances was difficult because these students did not stay in one school long enough to get to know the context and establish social networks. What the findings show is that as children, their schooling was negatively affected when they lost out on opportunities to gain membership to networks that could have facilitated their bonding with their peers which would have supported them with some of their educational challenges. They were functioning in school contexts that misrecognised the structural violence of poverty on their education by responding to them as if the educational playing fields were level. Absent from all three participants' lives was an informal network that consisted of parents or adults who understood the mechanics of the education system and who could interpret for these students how the system worked. The school as a social space had no place for resistant capital to grow and for the cultural injustices within the space to be challenged. As such, students like Hennie, Bronson and Karlien grew up internalising a belief that they were incapable of academic success.

When they entered the AETC they were exercising a second chance opportunity to gain the general education and training certificate. In my analysis of their educational experiences within AET, I found that adult students bring many dispositional constraints into the social space that stem from disempowering childhood experiences. However, whereas formal schooling misrecognised their societal challenges, the AET social space embraced it. My experiences of the AETCs were of spaces that were supportive and emancipatory. AET students described the spaces as non-threatening and where educators support, encourage and advise adults to complete their basic education. My findings confirm the agentic role of the AETC as represented by the AET culture, the facilitator actions and the pedagogical engagements. The AET facilitators were sensitised to the vulnerability of their adult student population and saw it as part of their educational role to be support students emotionally, socially and academically. AET facilitators were important social support networks for students. They mentored them and were important links to the formal and informal networks that students needed to be successful. In this educational space, the community cultural wealth (Yosso 2005) that adult students had accumulated in their lives were mined and upvalued through emancipatory pedagogies and actions by the educators. These adult educational spaces valued the aspirations, navigations, and resistances that adult students presented as alternative forms of capital to navigate student life. Moreover, the AET spaces' celebration of the forms of capital that their adult students have accumulated in life produced more critical readings of such knowledge's value in society. Thus, when these students entered AET they were inducted into a culture that promoted self-efficacy. The philosophy that guided AETC goals were that adult students are people of worth who have a contribution to make to society. In this type of environment, the three AET students experienced success and found their educational purpose in life.

References

Aitchinson JJW. 2003. Struggle and compromise: a history of Adult Basic Education from 1960 to 2001. *Journal of Education*, 29:123–178.

Andrews M, Squire C & Tambokou M (eds). 2008. *Doing narrative research*. London: Sage. https://doi.org/10.4135/9780857024992

Baatjes I. 2003.The new knowledge-rich society: perpetuating marginalisation and exclusion. *Journal of Education*, 29:179–204.

Bourdieu P. 1977. *Outline of a Theory of Practice*. Cambridge: Cambridge University Press. https://doi.org/10.1017/CBO9780511812507

Bourdieu P. 1986. "The forms of capital". In: J Richardson (ed). *Handbook of Theory and Research for the Sociology of Education*. New York: Greenwood. 241–258.

Bourdieu P. 1998. *Practical Reason: On the Theory of Action*. Cambridge, UK: Polity Press.

Bourdieu P & Passeron JC. 1977. *Reproduction in education, society and culture*, R Nice (trans). London: Sage.

Bourdieu P & Wacquant L. 1992. *An invitation to reflexive sociology.* Chicago: The University of Chicago Press.

Chase SE. 2005. "Narrative inquiry: Multiple lenses, approaches, voices". In: NK Denzin & YS Lincoln (eds). *The Sage handbook of qualitative research.* 3rd Edition. Thousand Oaks: Sage.

Creswell JW. 2003. *Research Design. Qualitative, Quantitative and Mixed Methods Approaches.* 2nd Edition. Thousand Oaks: Sage.

Cupchik G. 2001. Constructivist Realism: An Ontology That Encompasses Positivist and Constructivist Approaches to the Social Sciences. Forum: *Qualitative Social Research* 2(1), Art 7. http://nbn-resolving.de/urn:nbn:de:0114-fqs010177 [Accessed 20 February 2016].

Epstein JL. 2001. *School, Family, and Community Partnerships.* Boulder: Westview Press.

Henderson AT & Mapp KL. 2002. *A new wave of evidence: The impact of school, family, and community connections on student achievement.* Austin: Southwest Educational Development Laboratory.

Fataar A. 2008. "Desire and subjectivity: Schooling the post-apartheid city". Keynote Speech delivered at the Annual Postgraduate Students conference. University of Cape Town.

Fraser N. 2009. *Scales of Justice: Reimagining Political Space in a Globalizing World.* New York: Columbia University Press.

Harvey J. 2012. *Young Men in Prison: Surviving and adapting to life inside.* 2nd Edition. New York: Routledge.

Holt D. 1998. "Does cultural capital structure American consumption?" In: J Schor & D Holt (eds). *The consumer society reader.* NewYork: The New York Press. 212–252. https://doi.org/10.1086/209523

Jeynes WH. 2007. The Relationship Between Parental Involvement and Urban Secondary School Student Academic Achievement: A Meta-Analysis. *Urban Education,* 42(1):82–110. https://doi.org/10.1177/0042085906293818

Johnson HB. 2015. *The American dream and the power of wealth: Choosing schools and inheriting inequality in the land of opportunity.* New York: Routledge.

Josselson R. 2006. Narrative research and the challenge of accumulating knowledge. *Narrative Inquiry,* 16(1):3–10. https://doi.org/10.1075/ni.16.1.03jos

Lafferty L, Treloar C, Butler T, Guthrie J & Chambers GM. 2016. Social capital strategies to enhance hepatitis C treatment awareness and uptake among men in prison. *Journal of Viral Hepatitis,* 24(2):111–116. https://doi.org/10.1111/jvh.12627

Lareau A. 1989. *Home Advantage.* New York: Falmer.

Lareau A. 2002. Invisible Inequality: Social Class and Childrearing in Black Families and White Families. *American Sociological Review,* 67(5):747–776. https://doi.org/10.2307/3088916

Lareau A & Weininger EB. 2003. Cultural capital in educational research: A critical assessment. *Theory and Society*, 32:567–606. https://doi.org/10.1023/B:RYSO.0000004951.04408.b0

Liamputtong P & Ezzy D. 2005. *Qualitative Research Methods*. Oxford: Oxford University Press.

Ling C & Dale A. 2014. Agency and social capital: characteristics and dynamics. *Community Development Journal*, 49(1):4–20. https://doi.org/10.1093/cdj/bss069

Mertens D. 2014. *Research and Evaluation in Education and Psychology: Integrating Diversity with Quantitative, Qualitative, and Mixed Methods*. Thousand Oaks: Sage.

Mezirow J. 2000. "Learning to Think like an Adult. Core Concepts of Transformation Theory". In: J Mezirow & Associates (eds). *Learning as Transformation. Critical Perspectives on a Theory in Progress*. San Francisco: Jossey-Bass. 3–33.

Moerbeek H & Flap H. 2008. "Social Resources and Their Effect on Occupational Attainment through the Life Course". In: N Lin & BH Erickson (eds). *Social Capital: An International Research Program*. Oxford: Oxford University Press. https://doi.org/10.1093/acprof:oso/9780199234387.003.0064

Nash R. 1990. Bourdieu on Education and Social and Cultural Reproduction. *British Journal of Sociology of Education*, 11(4):431–447. https://doi.org/10.1080/0142569900110405

Patton, MQ. 2002. *Qualitative Research and Evaluation Methods*. Thousand Oaks: Sage.

Putnam RD. 2000. *Bowling alone: The collapse and revival of American Community*. New York: Simon & Schuster Paperbacks. https://doi.org/10.1145/358916.361990

Republic of South Africa. Department of Correctional Services. 2005. *White Paper on Corrections in South Africa*. Pretoria: Government Publishers.

Republic of South Africa. Department of Education. 2000. *Adult Basic Education and Training Act (Act 52 of 2000)*. Pretoria: Government Publishers.

Republic of South Africa. Department of Higher Education. 2013. *The White Paper on Post-School Education*. Pretoria: Government Publishers.

Republic of South Africa. UMALUSI. 2016. *Efficacy Research Project Report*. Pretoria.

Rule P. 2006. "The time is burning": The rights of adults to basic education in South Africa. *Journal of Education*, 39:113–135.

Rocco L & Suhrcke M. 2012. *Is social capital good for health? A European perspective*. Denmark: WHO Regional Office for Europe.

Rose D, Clear TR, Waring E & Scully K. 2000. "Coercive Mobility and Crime: Incarceration and Social Disorganisation" (unpublished manuscript).

Sampson RJ, Raudenbush SW & Earls F. 1997. Neighborhoods and Violent Crime: A Multilevel Study of Collective Efficacy. *Science*, 277:918–924. https://doi.org/10.1126/science.277.5328.918

Solórzano D & Yosso T. 2002. Maintaining social justice hopes within academic realities: a Freirean approach to critical race/LatCrit pedagogy. *Denver Law Review*, 78(4):595–621.

Trahar S. 2009. Beyond the Story Itself: Narrative Inquiry and Autoethnography in Intercultural Research in Higher Education. *Forum Qualitative Sozialforschung*, 10(1), Art 30. http://nbn-resolving.de/urn:nbn:de:0114-fqs0901308 [Accessed February 2016].

Terre Blanche M, Durrheim K & Painter D. 2006. *Research in Practice: Applied Methods for the Social Sciences*. 2nd Edition. Cape Town: UCT Press.

Yosso T. 2005. Whose culture has capital? A critical race theory discussion of community cultural wealth. *Race, Ethnicity and Education*, 8(1):69–91. https://doi.org/10.1080/1361332052000341006

Zipin L, Fataar A & Brennan M. 2015. Can Social Realism do Social Justice? Debating the Warrants for Curriculum Knowledge Selection. *Education as Change*, 19(2): 9–36. https://doi.org/10.1080/16823206.2015.1085610

Chapter 8

"The writing's on the wall … and in other forbidden places": Youth using languaging practices to mediate the past in formal and informal learning spaces

Adam Cooper

Me and my PhD research in the after-life

Research projects usually contain a 'before', a 'during' and an 'after'. This chapter is firmly located in the 'after-life' of my doctoral research, a period that has been incredibly productive for looking at what I did in new ways, in conversation with colleagues who have used different conceptual approaches. My PhD explored a language and a place, neither of which I fully understand. I was not raised speaking this language, or living in this place. The language could be called Kaapse Afrikaans, an informal version of Afrikaans. I have called the place 'Rosemary Gardens'[1] to protect the identities of the people whose words I 'took' or 'documented', depending on how you interpret these things. I worked with young people in Rosemary Gardens partly because it made me feel better about myself, that I was atoning for my whiteness. Also because I learnt about myself, the places that I live in and the divisions between myself and others through this work. As a researcher working for the Extra-Mural Education Project (EMEP), a position I held while completing my PhD, I will never forget how students at schools I visited would ask me: "Uncle, what country are you from?" The only white people they saw were German and American volunteers; it was unfathomable to them that I could have been born 10 kilometres away from where they lived, and that we shared a city, a nationality, a continent.

Working for EMEP in South African townships in the Western Cape between 2008 and 2012 changed me. Fundamentally. I had travelled on the National highway adjacent to many of these areas since I was a young boy, but this act of driving past does not give one a sense of how people based in township areas live. How they eat and wash and go to school. While trying to understand a violently different set of life circumstances from my own, I cobbled together a piece of research that was partly about me, partly about the young people I listened to and partly about the city we live in. Or perhaps

---

1   All the names of people, places and organisations are pseudonyms.

I should say 'cities', because my city and theirs overlapped, but it also contained independent regions, like two intersecting circles in a Venn diagram.

While conducting my research I was based in an academic department in which scholars often spoke about young people being blessed with 'assets' and 'funds' and 'capitals' and 'resources'. I became cynical in that this was very politically correct, very 'child-centred' and 'voice-giving'. My discomfort was bound up in the fact that those of us who oppose deficit approaches to schooling and resist perspectives that assume that poor students of colour are somehow inadequate, often lament that young people are well-endowed with forms of social capital, yet we rarely try to describe these substantively. In an attempt to resolve my dis-ease I looked for these funds, assets and capitals. I mainly listened for them. I spent a lot of time in classrooms and hanging around in community spaces in Rosemary Gardens, listening. I listened because I believe this simple practice is one of the most potent tools that researchers have at their disposal. I found a complex, rich set of artefacts, resources that were fundamental to how young people *did* learning: their words. To be honest I didn't really 'find' them. The colonisers did not 'find' Africa. It, and they, were there long before I started spending time at schools on the Cape Flats. But I have temporarily relocated these languaging practices in order to try to make a point as best I can, with the resources that are available to me. Let me first describe a few of those.

Languaging practices, mediation and misrecognition

My research took the form of a multi-site ethnography that compared how young people used language to learn in classrooms in comparison to how they were able to use language in informal educational places, namely a youth hip-hop group and a radio show. In this chapter I contrast the hip-hop crew with learning and language use at school. Rather than conceptualising language as a static, bounded, discrete entity with fixed grammar, vocabulary and syntax, I theorise that languaging practices are resources used to perform communicative actions in specific contexts (Blommaert 1999; Canagarajah 2013; McGroaty 2010; Pennycook 2007). Mass migration and increased contact between people in the era of globalisation has explicitly demonstrated that people use language in ways that transcend what has been understood as 'individual languages' and that they use signs and symbols that are not restricted only to using words. While these communicative practices have become more apparent in the global era, language mixing is a natural component of all inter-group contact and has occurred in many times and places, for example through colonial conquests (Canagarajah 2013; Luke 2005).

In this chapter, youth languaging practices are conceptualised as a form of mediation, an embodied practice that reveals how speech is materially infused in the city of Cape Town, mediating between past and present. Young people's words are the chrystalised material legacy, the residue produced by the intermingling of colonial Dutch and British settlers, indigenous groups like the Khoi and San, and imported slaves from East Africa and South Asia (Battersby 2003; Erasmus 2005; McCormick 2002).

The concept of the 'mediant' provides an alternative, more fluid and aggregated way of understanding the relationship between human beings and the worlds they inhabit, in comparison to binaries like 'structure-agency', 'individual-social' or 'objective-subjective' (Appadurai 2015). Rather than acting on their environment in a mechanistic fashion, mediants form part of dynamic assemblages that we might call 'systems', such as the education system. The concept 'mediant'; enables an analysis of the socialities that are produced in, with, and through particular materialities, illuminating a more nuanced representation of human life, in comparison to the overly purposive, insufficiently social idea of 'agency' (Appadurai 2015).

Through their languaging practices youth mediate between the past and present, between different parts of society, between the social order we accept without questioning and that which is submerged, pushed away, forgotten. Speech is one potent material product that sublimates through the iterative mediation process. The speech that youth in this study used at home and with friends differed substantially from the standardised Afrikaans that they learnt and were expected to use at school, a language which is a constitutionally protected product attached to the white Afrikaner political project.

The speech of Rosemary Gardens youth was not *recognised* as an authentic, valuable resource in classrooms in this neighbourhood. Pierre Bourdieu (1979, 1991) and Nancy Fraser (1999, 2000) have both used the concept of 'misrecognition', albeit is different ways, to describe how social injustice is produced and reproduced. This term is useful for exploring how the languaging practices of youth in my study were enabled, suppressed and appraised. For Bourdieu, misrecognition needs to be understood in relation to the education system more broadly and the ways in which knowledge operates in educational fields. The French word used by Bourdieu, 'connaisance' (recognition), implies a form of knowledge that is not merely the acquisition of facts, but is a far more embodied epistemological process that includes tacit knowledge, or 'knowing how' in particular fields. Bourdieu's concept of habitus, a fairly stable set of class and culturally formed dispositions, is intimately connected to this way of knowing. Misrecognition then, or 'meconnaisance', refers to a social process of misattribution, of subjects not "knowing how" in particular social situations or contexts. Misrecognition serves to justify the existing social order, as the supposed incompetence of not knowing how to perform social practices in particular fields is evidence of educational inferiority, which is in turn attributed to deficiency. It is easy to see the relationship between this process and linguistic ideologies, the ways that certain forms of speaking, using language and communication are understood to hold more social worth than others, functioning as self-justificatory evidence for existing hierarchies.

While Bourdieu's (1979, 1991) 'meconaissance' is bound up in how society attributes evaluative criteria to sets of cultural resources, practices and ontological dispositions, validating existing social hierarchies, Fraser's concern is with the micro dynamics that enable or inhibit participation in social interactions and which perpetuate forms of injustice. For Fraser (1999, 2000), misrecognition relates to institutionally shaped restrictions that curtail full participation in social processes. In other words, misrecognition refers to institutionalised rules for engagement that limit the participation of members of specific groups. While Bourdieu focuses on how practices and ways of being in the world are systematically interpreted and placed in a hierarchy, such that differences appear to be naturalised, Fraser delves into how hierarchy and power make practices possible for some people and not for others in the first place. Both forms of misrecognition contain a great deal of overlap and should be seen as complementary. Societal evaluations of practices and dispositions impact on whether it becomes possible to use these resources in meaningful social situations.

Integrating these ideas with the concept of mediation and the ways that students use language in educational settings, my research in Rosemary Gardens explored how mediation and misrecognition worked differently in formal and informal education places through the ways that they enabled young people to act as semiotically infused place-based mediators. The appraisal mechanisms used to assess youth languaging practices were integral to their being recognised as legitimate participants in educational sites. More detail on the two sites and the neighbourhood that form the focus of this chapter is provided in the next section and contextualising descriptions of the young people's languaging practices are provided thereafter.

Rosemary Gardens High School and the Doodvennootskap

Rosemary Gardens was established in the mid-1970s when people that the apartheid state classified as 'coloured' were removed from the inner city and parts of the suburbs and dumped in this neighbourhood. The vast majority of the people who were brought to this area, and who continue to live in it, speak a language variety that may be called Kaapse (Cape) Afrikaans or simply Kaaps.

I say 'classified by the apartheid state as coloured' intentionally. I am not a member of this group and do not intend to speak on behalf of its members. However, it would be impossible for me to analyse the relationship between language, social status and educational processes without making reference to the complex and fraught racial dynamics that have existed in the city of Cape Town and South Africa more generally. So let me provide a little more context. According to Adhikari (2005), the identity 'coloured' emerged in the aftermath of South Africa's precious mineral revolution as intense inter-group conflict occurred and people fought for employment. The group that had lived at the Cape through Dutch and British colonial rule asserted a separate identity as 'coloured', independent from Bantu speaking people. Later, during apartheid, the category 'coloured' was often rejected either in favour of a united racial opposition to the draconian government, in the form of Black Consciousness, or it was abandoned in favour of non-racialism. However, many coloured people themselves continued to self-identify with this category. Erasmus describes colouredness as:

> Cultural identities comprising detailed bodies of knowledge, specific cultural practices, memories, rituals and modes of being. Coloured identities were formed in the colonial encounter between colonists (Dutch and British), slaves from East and South India and from East Africa and conquered indigenous peoples, the Khoi and the San. This encounter and the power relations embedded in it have resulted in processes of cultural dispossession, borrowing and transformation. The result has been a highly specific and recognisable cultural formation – not just a 'mixture' but a very particular mixture comprising elements of Dutch, British, Malaysian, Indonesian, South East Asian and West African, Khoi, free Black and other forms of African culture appropriated, translated and articulated in complex and subtle ways. These elements acquire their specific cultural meaning only once fused and translated. (2001:21)

This diverse, forced meeting of peoples meant that it was common for up to five languages to be spoken in an 18th-century Cape Colony household (McCormick 2002). However, as time passed, interesting new contextually specific languaging practices began to emerge, linked to the material realities of the Cape. These languaging practices, most of which are now recognised as forms of Afrikaans, are heavily mediated by race, class and geography. The young people described in the study lived in an area formed during apartheid's forced removals, when people classified by the state as 'coloured' were forced to relocate from the inner city and suburbs to the newly created area called Rosemary Gardens. The version of Afrikaans spoken by these young people differs substantially from the standardised, white tainted version of the language that has been installed in the constitution and which is taught in the school curriculum. 'Kaapse' Afrikaans is often pejoratively perceived in the public imaginary as the language of the downtrodden and the *dronklap* (the drunkard), of the clowns and coons, the *skollies* (ruffians) and taxi queens, the addict, alcoholic and artisan. Social connotations that are infused with this language do not lend it to being associated with the erudite, learned scholar (Willemse 2013).

Moving on to the high school, Rosemary Gardens High School (RGHS) was founded in the late 1970s and has benefited from stable leadership over its 35-year existence, as the school has only ever had two principals. Recent changes in the school include the establishment of an after-school programme that consists of sports, music, dance and extra lessons for the students. These after-school activities were implemented through a partnership with the provincial government's Department of Cultural Affairs and Sports. Other changes that occurred after 2005 are the first school-community gym in South Africa being opened by Virgin Active on the school premises, a library that was built by the non-governmental organisation (NGO) Equal Education, a number of entrepreneurial ventures including farming lavender in order to produce cosmetics, and a bicycle workshop that operates from the school premises. Despite the school suffering from the effects of many of the social problems that plagued the local community, including gang violence, substance abuse and poverty, a number of promising initiatives existed in and around the school itself, leading many people to believe that the school was undergoing something of a renaissance.

The Doodvennootskap (DVS) hip-hop crew was an organically formed group of peers who established a number of relationships in Rosemary Gardens, most notably with a local NGO called the Children's Rights and Anti-Abuse Group (CRAAG). The group's relationship with CRAAG provided three members of the DVS group with employment and led to the group being allocated an office in the local community centre. This office provided the DVS group with access to a range of material benefits, such as the use of the internet and a telephone line, and they came into contact with a range of government officials and other personnel who moved though this space. DVS consisted of six to eight young men who met regularly in the office at the community centre and spent a great deal of time at each others' houses, writing lyrics, discussing strategy and recording tracks of their music. The DVS crew performed at various venues in the community and at hip-hop events elsewhere in the city. Through CRAAG they also conducted research on youth participation and 'youth voice' in Rosemary Gardens. While being influenced by concepts and ideas from global hip-hop discourses, for example ideas like striving to produce 'conscious' lyrics and 'keeping it real', members of DVS also emphasised the importance of validating local cultural artefacts. This background information provides something of a context in which to interpret the languaging practices of the youth at RGHS and amongst DVS.

Languaging practices at Rosemary Gardens High School

The first point that needs to be made in an analysis of Rosemary Gardens High School (RGHS) is that 400 Grade 9s and only 60 Grade 12s attended this institution in 2012. What this means is that RGHS had a discontinuation rate of over 400%. This appears to be a significant example of misrecognition, described by Fraser (2000) as the institutionally shaped restrictions that curtail full participation in social processes or institutionalised rules for engagement that limit participation. School discontinuation has been documented more generally at working-class coloured schools. The Cape Area Panel Study showed that while only 10% of students at schools in former Black African areas had left school by age 17, 40% of youth in areas previously reserved for coloured people had stopped attending school by the same age (Bray, Gooskens, Moses, Kahn & Seekings 2011).

Through interviews with teachers and students, I tried to understand how this process of misrecognition operated in the daily functioning of the school, contributing to students' decisions to stop attending. Some clues were provided by certain teachers' attitudes that the language that students spoke provided evidence of cultural deficiency, hindering their academic progress. To illustrate this point, one teacher said in an interview:

> The biggest problem is that learners come with a cultural deficiency ... no books at home. The only proper English or Afrikaans they hear is from the teachers. Their oral tradition is good, but we need to get them studying and reading. It's the basis of the education. Once they have good command of the language, they can be fine.

In this quotation, the teacher links students' supposed cultural deficiency to homes without books and 'improper' language usage. Rather than seeing the versions of Afrikaans that students spoke at home as **different** to the iteration of the language prescribed in the school curriculum, this teacher interpreted students' linguistic practices as evidence of cultural **deficiency**. It is interesting that this teacher recognised that the students had 'a good oral tradition', even though he stated that they arrived at school with a 'cultural deficiency' and no 'proper language'. It appears that he believed that while students' linguistic resources may be effectively utilised at home, they held little potential in educational contexts and that 'studying and reading' could only occur in standard or 'proper' languages. Pedagogical and learning-related activities occurring in his classroom were therefore proclaimed only to be possible through particular versions of language, meaning that he was required to act as a mediator in making these linguistic forms accessible. Similar debates have arisen in the United States in relation to African American Vernacular English (Delpit 1997).

This state of affairs, in which the students' linguistic resources were misrecognised as 'deficient', meant that the role of the students in the school context was reduced to one of a passive recipient of educators' cultural resources.

At RGHS, the value judgement that the young people did not speak a 'proper' language was extended to assumptions about students' values. Another educator said: "You can see by their accents that maybe my values and theirs doesn't merge because of their backgrounds." This educator said that the way that students spoke, in the form of their accents, was evidence of them also imbibing dubious values. Students' linguistic habitus was interpreted as linked to undesirable values, something which was deemed to be a result of their 'background'. The stereotypes of former coloured neighbourhoods as associated with criminality, illicit sexuality and substance abuse, were therefore evoked due to the ways in which teachers interpreted the social relevance of students' speech. These kinds of teacher attitudes indicate that they may have believed that it was undesirable to promote these young people's participation in the education system and mainstream society due to their supposed immoral tendencies.

Justifications for the existing social order were then made by the teachers with reference to class-based vocational tracks, a sentiment that further prevents working-class students from participating in the upper echelons of their society. The teacher quoted below was unable to see the value in intellectually rigorous forms of education for youth from Rosemary Gardens, instead favouring their participation in vocational education:

> This school should have a curriculum where some learners are taught to be plumbers, electricians, carpenters. That is one reason for the dropout rate. What school presents is not what the learner requires. Those are all careers where learners make a living. Why must we flog a dead horse?

Vocational education and training was suggested as more appropriate for working-class coloured youth from Rosemary Gardens, implying that these young people needed a less demanding intellectual programme. The reference to the dead horse is insulting to youth and highlights the lack of potential that some educators believed students had at their disposal. The reason for low participation in the school, especially in the later grades, was said to be a result of the mismatch between students' abilities and the academic programme of the school.

Some of the students at RGHS who remained in the school system and endured the hierarchical, institutionalised policies and practices that limited participation assimilated these ideas about the value of their cultural resources:

You can't mix your language. If I say 'no it's cool I'm going to chill in the sun', we can't speak like that. Your marks go down immediately. They will penalise you [repeats in English], they will penalise you.   [Translated from Afrikaans]

The student stated that the language practices that they utilised outside of the classroom were 'mixed', in comparison to the historically white version of Afrikaans, which was implied to be unmixed or pure. These youths learnt about the hierarchy of valuable language practices through evaluations of their academic work. Evaluation and feedback provided a powerful institutionalised practice that simultaneously demonstrated to students that if they were unable to assimilate and utilise the historically white version of Afrikaans, they would be unable to progress academically.

For many students who remained at school it was clear that linguistic appraisals were not simply based on educators and the school stating that equally valuable cultural forms existed, but that a distinct linguistic hierarchy was apparent:

It's a high standard of words that they use and we've got to get the terms right. Usually the teacher says to us … they will give it just so to us, but then they will try to make it easier for us. They give it just so and then they explain.
[Translated from Afrikaans]

And:

The words are very high this year. We never hear those kinds of words. Everything we get is in Afrikaans but it's high Afrikaans. Not the Afrikaans that we speak. It's a higher level. And that's the Afrikaans that they train us in. It's the Afrikaans that we ought to speak but it's not the Afrikaans that we speak.   [Translated from Afrikaans]

This student described how teachers enabled participation through 'dumbing down' academic work and making it easier for students to understand in the classroom. Participation was possible, but only on the terms prescribed by the school and its personnel. In this scenario the teacher mediated between the state, the school and its prescribed pedagogical practices, leaving the student as a passive object expected to mimic the language of the educator. In this way, the teacher highlighted a sociality that positioned students firmly at the bottom of the social hierarchy, with inadequate linguistic resources, dubious moral tendencies and limited potential. Their lack of familiarity with a prescribed set of random social practices used in a specific educational field was supposedly evidence of low intellectual ability and innate deficiency, 'a dead horse not worth flogging'.

At RGHS, culture and class-specific norms made certain ways of speaking appear to be evidence of inferiority, 'misrecognising' the value of the language that the students in Rosemary Gardens spoke. The social architecture of the classroom was designed to acknowledge the linguistic capitals of middle-class students through state-sanctioned language policies, inscribed in curricula, and educators who endorsed these standard language forms in their pedagogic practices. These policies and practices, as lived materialities of daily school life, affirmed certain ways of speaking as legitimate for formal education, communicating to students who conformed to these norms that they belonged and were more likely to excel in these places. The value placed on the languaging practices that working-class youth of colour had at their disposal inhibited their participation in educational discussions, written work and other activities that constituted school and classroom life. Not knowing how to communicate in the school context was therefore a result of the school defining which forms of language were designated to be of a high quality and able to be used for academic purposes, such as 'reading and studying'. These evaluative practices and policies limited the participation of Rosemary Gardens' youth at school, with many choosing not to attend school in the higher grades.

Student resistance to being oppressed in their use of language at school took on a range of forms, including the decision not to attend school. At RGHS, students wrote on every available surface and object; forms of graffiti were ubiquitous on the walls of the school, saturating school uniforms, desks and walls. The majority of the students walked around the school with their grey school trousers blotted with white correction fluid that proclaimed words and symbols, announcing messages between friends and names of peers in romantic relationships. In classrooms desks were chiselled with similar images and words. Denied the opportunity to use their language practices in classrooms, students reclaimed opportunities to do so by marking other material surfaces in the school.

A similar form of semiotic guerilla warfare was described by a member of the young hip-hop collective that I met at a community meeting on school dropout, a session that was hosted by a local NGO. The young men that formed part of this collective were powerfully outspoken at the meeting, voicing their opinions and disagreeing with others when appropriate. Their actions existed in stark contrast to a group of parent school governing body members who attended the meeting in silence. At this event, a young man, who I will call Fabio, described why he decided to stop attending RGHS in the following manner:

> When I'm at home I felt more stuff than I did at school because at school all I would do was read and write and not listen. I got bored after a while. Then

I just started writing poetry and that kind of stuff, and writing lyrics. When I'm at home I write better. When I'm at school I can't write because there's no activity or place for me to do that kind of stuff. So that was one of the, I can't say one of the main reasons, but yeah. I think I was the problem there, my mindset, where I was thinking.

Fabio's decision to discontinue his schooling was informed by the fact that he felt that, ironically, "there was no activity or place to do that kind of stuff" (writing). Surely the raison d'être of classrooms is to provide people with opportunities to read and write? So why did he feel that there was no place to write at school, but that he could write what and how he liked as part of DVS? The hip-hop crew's lyrics provide some insights into this question.

"My porridge bowl is *nou* [now] a satellite dish": languaging practices amongst DVS

When I listened to the lyrics that DVS wrote, predominantly in the form of an album which they sold, as well as at live performances, I noticed that the words that they uttered consisted of the same, unashamed language that the group spoke in other places. I also observed that they regularly made explicit references to the environments in which they lived, pointing out social phenomena and injustices. Consider the following examples of DVS lyrics:

1. Babies lost their toys *want* their *tannies wil* rattle.
   [Babies lost their toys because their mothers want to rattle.]

2. My porridge bowl is *nou* a satellite dish.
   [My porridge bowl is now a satellite dish.]

3. My self-confidence *se* boosters *het* bruises.
   [My self-confidence boosters have bruises.]

4. People *vat 'n* facebook post cause they wanna be the voice, *hulle dink hulle is die ou want hulle een* show host.
   [People take a facebook post because they want to be the voice, they think they are the man because they host one show.]

5. Decisions *word gemaak sonder ons en nou moet ek my bek hou, in* nowadays *se* status *baie mense kyk op na jou en jy's 'n* infection, you were born from a weak reaction.
   [Decisions are made without us and now I must shut my animalistic mouth, in nowadays status many people look up to you and you're an infection, you were born from a weak reaction.]

6. Instant pudding, instant *koffie*, instant *dood met 'n* once off guarantee.
   [Instant pudding, instant coffee, instant death with a once off guarantee.]

7. Organisations are competing, doing it for charity.

8. *Ek is* not *van* Bollywood or *van* Hollywood, *ek is* straight *uit die* skollyhood.
   [I am not from Bollywood or Hollywood, I am straight out of the skollyhood.]

Through their written lyrics, DVS showed that they had reflected and commented on the environments in which they lived. The first line above uses a clever pun to refer to parental neglect, as mothers are chastised for spending their resources on partying or 'rattling', rather than on toys for their children. Similarly, in line two, money that could have been spent on food is criticised as used for entertainment instead, in the form of satellite television. The third line is probably an allusion to drug use ('self-confidence boosters'), with 'bruises' implying that these substances cause physical and emotional pain.

In line four, the reference to 'facebook' and the 'voice' (a tabloid newspaper) is a comment on how forms of social media have now assumed the role of 'news', as individuals are narcissistically able to create their own personal shows. Line five states that decisions are made for young people and they are forced to shut their *'beks'* (a *bek* is the mouth of an animal). Even though some local residents revered DVS, they proclaimed themselves to be "an infection ... born from a weak reaction". This is a reference to racist stereotypes associated with themselves, with connotations of 'contamination, disease, impurity' and 'mixed' or 'diluted' origins.

In line six, instant products like 'coffee' and 'pudding', are placed alongside 'death', which is also perceived to be a common, cheap phenomenon. This observation is probably due to the widespread presence of gangs in Rosemary Gardens, which present dangers for young people and other residents.

The fact that supposedly altruistic organisations, namely NGOs, were operating in the neighbourhood, is critiqued in line seven as 'competing for charity', a paradoxical state of affairs that questions the real purpose of the 'NGO industrial complex' and the ways in which it purports to promote the interests of local community members. The final line uses the name of the album from which these lyrics appeared: 'Skollyhood'. A 'skolly' is a lower-class delinquent with dubious moral inclinations. 'Skollyhood' refers to the group's ambiguous position as local celebrities for young people from the area, but that they remained, in the general public perception, coloured boys from an area associated with gangsterism, school dropouts and substance abuse.

Through their written lyrics, the group was able to refer to social problems in their community and society, reflect on their racial and class-based identities and express some of their fears and emotional vulnerability. While students at RGHS said that they were punished for mixing language, DVS members did so unapologetically. In the first line, the young rapper appears to mix English and Afrikaans almost every alternate word. Rather than perceiving these young men's language as a form of a 'restricted code', it appears as if standard English or Afrikaans are restricted and that they elaborate on these uniform languages, creating new hybrid forms (Alim 2009). The school disallowed apparent linguistic 'mixing', however DVS, like other groups of young rappers elsewhere, operated within a different set of norms and rules. Through hip-hop, which is the biggest youth sub-culture globally, young people play with, rearrange, invert and mash up forms of language, challenging dominant norms and inverting linguistic rules at the intersections of global and local flows of communication (Alim 2009; Dimitriadis 2001; Perullo & Fenn 2003).

Many linguists now believe that all languages are mixtures from different sources and that languages evolve organically through the ways in which they are used in communicative practice. The idea of standardised versions of language is not established due to an inherent superior quality associated with certain versions; rather, it is used to uphold certain groups' cultural capital for political purposes. Standard languages emerged with modern nation states in Europe and the idea of 'one people, one territory, one language' served particular political purposes (Canagarajah 2013; Mesthrie, Swann, Deumert & Leap 2009). Standard languages are therefore political tools that do not necessarily have greater or lesser linguistic value than other versions (Blackledge & Pavlenko 2002; Gee 1990; Makoe & Mckinney 2014). Put another way, one version of a language is not more or less sophisticated, complex or scholarly than another. Rather, standard languages have been used by members of groups to justify and reproduce the social order (Collins 1989; Stubbs 2002).

Through their collective work as part of the DVS hip-hop crew, these young men did more than just speak as they did at home, defying the authority of the school in using what that institution would have called a form of 'mixed' language. DVS provided these young men with opportunities to engage with the environments in which they lived and comment on, for example poverty, food shortages, problematic recreational activities and gangsterism. Their critique extended beyond blaming members of their community. The lyrics also illustrated how these young men challenged stereotypes associated with themselves and their neighbourhood and questioned the value of the lives of the Rosemary Gardens residents.

DVS therefore provided these young people with opportunities to act as mediants who foregrounded social realities relevant to their lives. Through their rapping activities, the group highlighted the social conditions in which they lived and were able to use language, without being cast as incompetent and/or inferior. Unlike the school,

DVS empowered the group to make sense of their heritage and challenge dominant narratives linked to colonialism. As one group member said:

> A big thing at the school is that the misters/sirs don't kick off on the youngsters' level. There's always that 'I am the adult you are the learner'. 'I am right you are wrong.' If you say 'does sir know that Jan van Riebeeck isn't the man in the portrait?', then the sir is going to fight with him. In the sir's book it isn't so. His research and his intelligence which he learns in other places is on a different level. 'I am the sir, studied for 30 years to be the sir. Everything that you say doesn't matter.' So he can challenge the sir on certain aspects but the sir isn't going to give him credit for that. Because there's only one way in the sir or madam's mind. I am the adult, you the child. And that ties into my work. We don't want to permanently make decisions for the youth. We teach the youth that their voices have weight. Their opinions count. They can be part of the decision-making.
>
> [Translated from Afrikaans. In the original, the interviewee used the word 'meneer', which I have translated as 'sir'.]

In this statement a member of DVS described how it was not possible, in the school context, to engage in dialogue and refute knowledge of the curriculum presented by teachers that had attended prestigious educational institutions like universities. The example of Jan van Riebeeck is highly symbolic: van Riebeeck was the original Dutch colonial settler who is often somewhat offensively portrayed as the father of coloured people, he and his peers' 'relations' with indigenous Khoi and San interpreted as having given 'birth' to coloured offspring. Through his example above, the member of DVS stated that it was impossible to engage and explore his heritage and this history of colonial conquest in the school context, because educators are the sole legitimate mediants of this knowledge. At school, students' 'backgrounds' and linguistic resources were adjudicated to be 'deficient' and inappropriate for 'reading and studying' or for contributing to knowledge production in subjects like history. In comparison, DVS illustrated how these young people could not only use their language to write and learn, but they could do so in ways that challenged the kinds of knowledges which the school curriculum upheld.

Students as mediants: towards a social theory of schooling

So how do 'mediation', 'misrecognition' and 'languaging practices', help us to understand these young people and the educational processes they engage with in a manner that may be productive? As a starting point, the 'agency' of the young people described in this chapter does not emerge in relation or opposition to the 'structure', the material and social formations in which they exist. These young people, more particularly the words they use at school or in a rap group, are actually an ingrained part of the structure; their words are the material legacy of that structure. It is therefore more useful to state that youth are not trying to defeat or overcome the forces that exist in their worlds, they are operating such that they attempt to reveal and press against or resist those very forces, albeit in guise. These young people's spoken words are bound up in and the products of a set of material conditions made up by slavery, colonial expansion and the establishment of the Cape Colony, social circumstances that laid the foundation for modern-day South Africa. They are mediants of that history, living relics of those conditions and they refuse to let it be forgotten by the new South African state and its neoliberal aspirations for global competitiveness and reconciliatory rainbows. Rather than attempting to find ways to be resilient in difficult circumstances or succeeding against the odds, these youths want to show us different interpretations of those circumstances, a different configuration of odds. This is what Fabio meant when he said: "When I'm at school I can't write because there's no activity or place for me to do that kind of stuff."

There was no activity or place at school to do the kind of writing that was meaningful to him, that allowed him to act as a mediant between and for the material circumstances of which he is a product, and through which he could speak with legitimacy. There were places and activities for writing at the school, but those places 'told' him that his language was culturally deficient, that he was likely to commit crimes in the afternoons and that he was better suited to be a plumber or a carpenter, rather than a writer. As an institutional assemblage, the school communicated to Fabio that he needed to uplift and assimilate himself into the school culture in order to be respected and succeed in that environment. These institutional forces are younger relatives of the apartheid state apparatus and colonial projects that committed horrific injustices, consigning Fabio and his family to live in Rosemary Gardens, work in particular realms of employment and to accept racialised identities with distinct social significance. These young mediants were therefore misrecognised by the school, both through the ways in which their linguistic practices were inscribed with value and by the way in which their full participation was limited. In reaction to the school's suppression of their social resources, the students participated in other spatially sanctioned realms, like graffiting walls, desks and school uniforms, and they attended other informal educational groups in order to exercise their intellectual and linguistic faculties.

The relationship between mediation, misrecognition and the operations of language, therefore, illustrates one way in which a robust social theory of school knowledge may be developed. For a long time, South African education scholarship has been plagued by what Fataar (2016) calls a social-subjective divide in which academics either under- or over-theorise the social components of school knowledge dissemination. While 'oversocialised' scholarship utilises 'identity research' to ameliorate the harmful effects of South Africa's colonial and apartheid histories, undersocialised approaches draw on hard boundary, neo-Bersteinian pedagogical theories to keep the external noise of the home, community and cultural heritage at bay. A study of languaging practices may transcend this divide because language is indispensable both to 'who young people are' and to how they become armed with powerful knowledges. Languaging is an integral part of the pedagogic device and the embodied transfer of powerful knowledges, and it simultaneously mediates social stratifications through forms of misrecognition that denigrate young people's linguistic resources, positioning them within raced, classed and gendered social hierarchies. A more robust social understanding of how knowledge transfer occurs in schools, informed by socio-linguistic theory that takes history and power seriously, can therefore be obtained from research in out of school sites, which, when pedagogically connected to school learning, could buttress schools with a vigorous teaching platform to excite and engage their students in rich learning.

What comes after the after-life?

During my journey between Rosemary Gardens and the academy, a time when South Africa changed fundamentally as young people challenged the narrative of 'rainbows and reconciliation', I thought a great deal about this thing we call 'knowledge'. I regularly wondered about the differences between what we do in elite academic spaces and local forms of knowledge that young people produce in the course of daily life. I wondered how much of the difference relates to 'packaging', i.e. the way that we dress up forms of knowledge to masquerade as intelligent thought through using language to justify that we are 'educated'. I'm not exactly sure where my next adventure will take me and what I will learn from it. There would be little point to doing research if we already knew the answers prior to doing the work. But I suspect my next exploration will involve further attempts to tease out the relationship between the form and function of different types of knowledge, working with young people so that all involved can reflect on the differences between status and substance. I believe that this kind of work contributes to something which I would call 'education'.

References

Adhikari M. 2005. *Not White Enough, Not Black Enough: Racial Identity in the South African 'Coloured' Community*. Cape Town: Double Storey Books.

Alim HS. 2009. "Creating 'an Empire Within an Empire': Critical Hip Hop, Language Pedagogies and the Role of Sociolinguistics". In: HS Alim, A Ibrahim & A Pennycook (eds). *Global Linguistic Flows: Hip Hop Cultures, Youth Identities, and the Politics of Language*. London: Routledge. 213–230.

Appadurai A. 2015. Mediants, materiality, normativity. *Public Culture*, 27(2):221–237. https://doi.org/10.1215/08992363-2841832

Battersby J. 2003. "'Sometimes it feels like I'm not black enough': recast(e)ing coloured through South African hip hop as a postcolonial text". In: S Jacobs & H Wasserman (eds). *Shifting selves: post-apartheid essays on mass media, culture and identity*. Cape Town: Kwela Books. 109–129.

Blackledge A & Pavlenko A. 2002. Ideologies of Language in Multilingual Contexts: Special Issue. *Multilingua*, 21:2–3.

Blommaert J. 1999. "The Debate is Open". In: J Blommaert (ed). *Language Ideological Debates*. New York: Mouton De Gruyter. 1–38. https://doi.org/10.1515/9783110808049.1

Bourdieu P. 1979. Symbolic power. *Critique of anthropology*, 4(13–14):77–85. https://doi.org/10.1177/0308275X7900401307

Bourdieu P. 1991. *Language and Symbolic Power*. Cambridge: Polity Press.

Bray R, Gooskens I, Moses S, Kahn L & Seekings J. 2011. *Growing up in the new South Africa: Childhood and adolescence in post-apartheid Cape Town*. Cape Town: HSRC Press.

Canagarajah S. 2013. *Literacy as Translingual Practice: Between Communities and Classrooms*. New York: Routledge.

Collins J. 1989. Hegemonic Practice: Literacy and Standard Language in Public Education. *The Journal of Education*, 171(2):9–34. https://doi.org/10.1177/002205748917100203

Cooper A. 2017. *Dialogue in places of learning: youth amplified from South Africa*. London: Routledge.

Delpit L. 1997. Ebonics and Culturally Responsive Instruction: What Should Teachers Do? Rethinking Schools. Online, 12(1). http://www.Rethinkingschools.Org/Archive/12_1/Ebdelpit_Shtml [Accessed 13 June 2015].

Dimitriadis G. 2001. *Performing Identity/Performing Culture: Hip Hop as Text, Pedagogy, and Lived Practice*. New York: Peter Lang.

Erasmus Z. 2001. "Introduction: Re-Imagining Colored Identities in Post-Apartheid South Africa". In: Z Erasmus (ed). *Coloured by History, Shaped by Place: New Perspectives on Coloured Identities in Cape Town*. Cape Town: Kwela Books. 13–28.

Fataar A. 2016. Towards a humanising pedagogy through an engagement with the social-subjective in educational theorising in South Africa. *Educational Research for Social Change*, 5(1):10–21. https://doi.org/10.17159/2221-4070/2016/v5i1a1

Fraser N. 1999. "Social justice in the age of identity politics: Redistribution, recognition, and participation". In: L Ray & A Sayer (eds). *Culture and economy after the cultural turn*. London: Sage. 25–52. https://doi.org/10.4135/9781446218112.n2

Fraser N. 2000. Rethinking recognition. *New Left Review*, 3(May–June):107.

Gal S & Irvine J. 1995. The Boundaries of Languages and Disciplines: How Ideologies Construct Difference. *Social Research*, 967–1001.

Gee JP. 1990. *Sociolinguistics and Literacies: Ideologies in Discourse*. London: Falmer Press.

Luke A. 2005. "Foreword: On the Possibilities of a Post-Postcolonial Language Education". In: A Lin & P Martin (eds). *Decolonisation, Globalisation: Language in Education Policy and Practice*. Clevedon: Multilingual Matters. XIV–XIX.

Makoe P & McKinney C. 2014. Linguistic Ideologies in Multilingual South African Suburban Schools. *Journal of Multilingual and Multicultural Development*, 35(7):658–673. https://doi.org/10.1080/01434632.2014.908889

McCormick K. 2002. *Language in Cape Town's District Six*. Oxford: Oxford University Press.

McGroarty M. 2010. "The Political Matrix of Linguistic Ideologies". In: B Spolsky & F Hult (eds). *The Handbook of Educational Linguistics*. UK: Wiley-Blackwell. 98–112.

Mesthrie R, Swann J, Deumert A & Leap W. 2009. *Introducing Sociolinguistics*. Edinburgh: Edinburgh University Press.

Pennycook A. 2007. Language, Localization, and the Real: Hip Hop and the Global Spread of Authenticity. *Journal of Language, Identity, and Education*, 6(2):101–115. https://doi.org/10.1080/15348450701341246

Perullo A & Fenn J. 2003. "Language Ideologies, Choices, and Practices in Eastern African Hip Hop". In: H Berger & M Carroll (eds). *Global Pop, Local Language*. Mississippi: University Press of Mississippi. 19–51.

Stubbs M. 2002. "Some Basic Sociolinguistic Concepts". In: L Delpit & J Dowdy (eds). *The Skin that we Speak: Thoughts on Language and Culture in the Classroom*. New York: The New Press. 63–86.

Willemse H. 2013. Obituary: Jakes Gerwel (1946–2012). *Tydskrif vir Letterkunde*, 50(1): 126–131. https://doi.org/10.4314/tvl.v50i1.10

Chapter 9

Prompting students' learning dispositional adaptation in response to teachers' pedagogical practices in a township school

Jennifer Feldman

Introduction

This chapter provides a discussion on student learning dispositions within the context of a township primary school in the Western Cape. By student learning dispositions I refer to students' orientation towards their learning as well as the manner in which they engage with learning opportunities. The chapter is situated within the current South African schooling discourse and complexity of student learning in impoverished spaces. It discusses how teachers and students, within a practice-based research process, came to mediate alternate learning practices.

The research process on which this chapter is based was twofold and included a professional learning community (PLC) involving six teachers and a weekly focus group of six Grade 6 students. The chapter discussion, based on the research data, makes no claim to the generalisability of the student learning practices and teachers' adapted pedagogy. What it intends rather, is to provide a window of understanding into the dynamics and complexity of student learning dispositions and school learning in impoverished spaces. Related to this, and the focus of the chapter discussion, is the possibility of teachers enriching student learning dispositions by working with student identities, knowledges and literacies from their homes and communities, and connecting these into school curriculum units to mediate different, more engaging and enriched student learning.

The premise on which the need for an adapted approach to teaching and learning is based, is found in the current South African schooling discourse that is described as scripted and regulated by the Department of Education. What this means for schools in low-income environments, such as township school contexts, is that the current educational policy, which is based on the Curriculum and Assessment Policy Statement (CAPS), tends to tightly frame and regulate how teachers teach and how students learn. However, this ignores or misrecognises the diversity of students and the social-cultural contexts in which schooling takes place. This discourse positions township schools, and by default teachers and students, within a regime of compliance and conformity that narrowly constrains the manner in which teaching and learning take place.

What this chapter brings into view, is how teachers in a township school context adapted their pedagogies to mediate a more socially just approach to teaching and learning. This approach, drawing on Fraser's conceptualisation of a socially just orientation, considered ways in which the teachers could join the redistribution of knowledge with an ethical consideration "for *recognition* of diverse cultural knowledge, and a *representation* of diverse of the social-cultural groups in processes of knowledge selection" (Zipin, Fataar & Brennan 2015, italics in original). The PLC dialogue, therefore, centred on finding ways to shift the way in which teachers redistributed the knowledge code to recognise student practices and literacies in order to more deeply connect and engage their students in school learning.

The data for the chapter is constructed from a twelve-month practice-based research project. As a participant researcher on the project, I was positioned as the facilitator of a teacher PLC and student focus group. Besides meeting with the students weekly I also spent time observing and engaging with the students in the classroom. As a white middle-aged researcher observing and engaging in a predominantly black African township school environment with young novice teachers and isiXhosa speaking students, my positioning in the practice-based research project was not without complication. Therefore, within the chapter narrative, I include reflective comments as a researcher regarding my involvement in the unfolding practice-based research process with the teachers and students.

The structure of the chapter begins by providing a rationale for a practice-based research process and includes a discussion on the research methodology. This section includes an explanation of the role that the PLC played in leveraging the teachers' pedagogical adaptations in order to engage students in their learning via a recognition and representation of the students' socially generated knowledge in the process of school knowledge redistribution. Secondly, the chapter discusses the township school context where the practice-based research took place. Thirdly, and the main focus of the chapter, is a discussion based on the empirical data from the student focus group and classroom observation that describes how the six students' learning dispositions shifted and changed as the teachers, over time, came to adapt and enrich their modes of pedagogical transfer and student learning. The chapter concludes by discussing the potential for shifting or changing the 'terms of recognition' (Appadurai 2004) on which student learning is founded to engage with the meanings and values, the 'lived and feeling' (Williams 1977) aspects of students' learning dispositions. This allows for school learning to resonate with the identities, knowledges, practices and literacies of all students within the schooling context.

Rationale and methodology

The South African education system, despite numerous policy reforms post-apartheid, has struggled to raise the level of education across the country. South Africa remains near the bottom of international assessments in systemic measures of performance such as the Progress in International Reading and Literacy Study (PIRLS) and Trends in International Mathematics and Science Study (TIMSS). The Annual National Assessment (ANA) scores are equally low and consistent with the low international measures of the performance of South African students. In response to these poor levels of student achievement in South Africa, as well as the immense diversity found in the South African schooling system, the current educational reform, namely the Curriculum and Assessment Policy Statement (CAPS) was implemented in 2011. The CAPS, described as a 'back to basics' approach (Sayed & Motala 2012:113), is aimed at shifting the curriculum policy focus to a controlled transfer of knowledge and learning in an attempt to meet the basic educational needs of all students. The proponents of the 'back to basics' approach argue that the policy innovations and changes made post-apartheid introduced interventions that did not support teaching and learning. They posit that many post-apartheid innovations and changes have in fact destabilised the education system by introducing interventions that are not well suited to the poor (Sayed & Motala 2012:113–114).

Described as tightly scripted and regulated (Fataar 2015), the CAPS is based on a mode of teaching that prescribes the specifics of content, pace and pedagogy in order to make curricular knowledge visible and explicit to all students. In reality, what CAPS does, is reduce teaching and learning to a set of basic knowledge codes that makes no allowance for students' different educational practices, knowledge and interests. Sayed and Motala argue that a curriculum that is stripped down to the essentials "may result in modest and temporary gains", but is unlikely to bring about any deep-seated transformation of teaching and student learning (2012:114). Further, Sayed and Motala state that rather than an "inherently biased and narrowly utilitarian" approach to education, such as is found in the current CAPS, "what the poor need instead are varied and challenging curricula and forms of pedagogy that suit their particular context and circumstances" (2012:114).

Hattam, Brennan, Zipin and Comber (2009) explain that school learning tends to align to the cultural arbitrary of middle-class student dispositions and knowledge. Students whose embodied capital or habitus does not match the requirements of the school code struggle to draw connections between their home- or community-based learning experiences and those of their school learning. Discussing the current CAPS, Harrop-Allin and Kros (2014:85) state that the way in which knowledge is presented in the CAPS with respect to the subjects History and Social Studies, tends to be in the form of "random, isolated, decontextualized elements". What this means is that students whose embodied capital and knowledge does not align with the cultural arbitrary of the middle-class school code struggle to make meaningful connections with their school learning.

Discussing the role that cultural and social capital play in positioning students within the schooling context, Bourdieu (1984) states that students enter schooling from different structural positions due to early-life immersion in the family and communities that embody distinctive qualities of dispositions or 'habitus'. Bourdieu (1984) describes the 'primary habitus' as repetitive patterns of practice and interaction from early childhood that have been internalised within our family. These social habits are based on ways of knowing from our family positions, economic class and other structural power relations that emerge in different contexts (see Zipin & Brennan 2006). For students living and attending schools in impoverished township contexts these 'ways of knowing' are often founded on a set of practices that do not align with the traditional school knowledge code.

As students navigate their social spaces by moving from their home-based settings to school sites, "children begin acquiring overlays of what Bourdieu calls 'secondary habitus' (1977) as they assimilate experiential affects of new conditions into the dispositional scaffolding of primary habitus" (Zipin & Brennan 2006). Schools are meant to facilaitate this habitus shift via engaging students in learning processes that facilitate secondary habitus acquisition, i.e. processes that educate students to develop new knowledge conceptions. Bourdieu explains that one's habitus is a composite of multiple dispositions; it is also always individual and one's habitus will embody codes that it senses as a familiar identity and in turn will make a distinction to that which it is less familiar with, considering them as 'others' (Bourdieu 1984). The degree of this secondary assimilation by students, via their learning at school, will therefore depend "on whether the codes of pedagogical interaction, and other institutional features of schooling, are reasonably near, or far, from what primary habitus senses as familiar" (Zipin & Brennan 2006).

Bourdieu states that educational systems, and especially schools, reproduce social stratification by maintaining:

> ... the pre-existing order, that is, the gap between pupils endowed with unequal amounts of cultural capital ... by a series of selection operations, the system separates the holders on inherited cultural capital from those who lack it. Differences in aptitude being inseparable from social differences according to inherited capital, the system thus tends to maintain pre-existing social differences. (1998:20)

Students whose embodied cultural capital or habitus aligns with the school system are enabled by the school to access the codes of schooling while others without such capital are denied the opportunity to achieve success at school or feel that school is in their best interests. These students find that the curriculum makes little connection to the learning from their community contexts or lifeworld knowledges and, therefore, they see no intrinsic value in engaging with the educational experience.

The practice-based research project that informs this chapter consisted of working with six teachers in a PLC to find ways in which the teachers could work with the identities, practices, knowledge and literacies of their students in the design and implementation of the school curriculum units. This approach is aimed at recognising the students' lifeworld ways of knowing, scaffolding these into the learning process to create a pedagogically responsive curriculum by which diverse students can thrive in mainstream institutions. This process challenges a deficit theorising approach that blames the underachievement of minority and low-income students as "a plethora of inadequacies, such as inadequate home literacy practices, inadequate English language, inadequate motivation, inadequate parental support and inadequate self-concept" (Hogg 2011:666).

In order for the teachers to work towards an adapted pedagogical platform, the PLC process operated via repeated iterations of experimentation, implementation and reflection. The teachers experimented with teaching strategies that invited their students to become actively engaged in their school learning, as opposed to passive knowledge receivers, by connecting their lifeworld knowledge into school learning practices. The practice-based research project included myself, as a university-based researcher who facilitated the PLC dialogue, the six PLC teachers and six Grade 6 students who were involved in focus-group discussions. This chapter presents a narrative account of the adaptive pedagogical process and the students' learning dispositions from the data collected over a twelve-month period.

Context for the research project

The school where the research took place is situated in a township on the Cape Flats in the Western Cape. The area can be described as consisting of impoverished living conditions where most families are living and working to survive on a daily basis. As a relatively newly developed area, Duduza (pseudonym) was established in 2004 as part of an integrated housing project that relocated coloured and black African families, as part of the Reconstruction and Development Programme (RDP)[1] housing project, from nearby informal settlements. Duduza Extension, where the school is situated, was built as a sub-section of Duduza to accommodate an additional 2400 households. Over the past ten years, this area has grown substantially and now encompasses approximately 10000 households, and as a result the current schooling infrastructure is unable to accommodate all the students in the area. In 2011 Duduza had a population of 45000 living in 10520 households (Statistics South Africa 2011). Many families do not enjoy formal or permanent employment and the unemployment rate in 2011 for this area was 37.9% (Statistics South Africa 2011). Duduza can be described as an impoverished township environment with a myriad of social issues which impact directly on the youth in the area.

Duduza Primary School was built to accommodate 1200 students but, as no further schools have been built in the area, the school receives far more applications for students to attend than it can accommodate. Due to this the principal fights hard to maintain a class size under 45 students. Despite Duduza being an integrated area, most of the students at the school are isiXhosa speaking. However, the language of instruction in the school from Grade 4 upwards is English, which undoubtedly adds a level of complexity to student learning practices. The school is a no-fee school and relies solely on government funding. The school runs a National Schools Nutrition Programme that is provided for by the government due to severe poverty in the area.

The PLC teachers felt that the dire social conditions of the area impacted significantly on the expectations of what their students could achieve. One PLC teacher noted:

> If this school and these students were not here in this context, the results would be very different. The context of where the students come from makes a big difference to what people expect from the students. We have to do something different because I believe in the students and I believe they can

---

1   The RDP housing project was an initiative of the South African socio-economic policy framework implemented by the African National Congress (ANC) government in 1994. The chief aim of the policy was to address the immense socio-economic problems, specifically the shortfalls in social services across the country, which existed due to the apartheid regime.

achieve the same marks as those schools in good areas. We have to find a way to do it, in this context and in this school. There must be a way.

It was the teachers' concern for their students' ongoing under-achievement and their desire to find a way to encourage their students to become active and passionate students that led to the establishment of the PLC in the school. The starting point for the PLC conversation was the teachers' belief that if they collaborated and dialogued together, they could find ways to affect pedagogical change that in turn could shift and change their students' learning dispositions. The PLC discussion, therefore, focused on finding ways in which the teachers could enrich their teaching and learning process by adapting their pedagogy to include their students' lifeworld knowledge and interests into the school curriculum.

Students' assemblages of learning

The six Grade 6 students, three boys and three girls, whose learning assemblages form the focus of this chapter, live in what can be described as a constrained or multi-deprived (Maringe, Masinire & Nkambule 2015) social environment. By learning assemblages, I refer to the different elements of students' learning, both within the formal structure of schooling as well as learning from their home and community contexts. Together these comprise the learning identities or dispositions of the students.

The six students live with their parents or extended family members in Duduza RDP houses. Those whose parents are employed travel substantial distances outside of Duduza to their places of employment, leaving home early in the morning and returning by 19h00 in the evening. The students are required to assist with household chores and look after their younger siblings until their parents return from work. The students describe their afternoon activities as a time where they socialise and play games with their friends in the street in which they live. The school does not usually require them to complete homework tasks as, according to the teachers, "most of them never do the work and there is just not enough time in class for checking and marking homework" (PLC conversation). The students say that they sometimes take their books home and study the work they did in class, though in general, a culture of studying beyond the formal school day is not evident among the students. Before exams, however, the six students state that they spend time studying in the evenings once their parents are home, but at least three of the students in the group confess that they find studying at home very difficult.

The six students who formed the focus group all firmly believed that being successful in school would enable them to achieve their goals of studying further in order that they, one day, may have a good job. For these students, believing in the possibility of a successful life was essential as it provided the impetus for them to stay at school. The students state that if they do not do well in school they do not know what will happen in the future. One of the students stated that "if you don't work hard, you can drop out, do drugs, get drunk, then the gangs get hold of you and the girls get pregnant" (student discussion). They recognise, therefore, that unless they can achieve in their school studies, the alternative is social and cultural reproduction that could potentially hold them captive in a cycle of ongoing poverty.

For the students, aspirations for the future included earning enough money that would enable them and their families to move out of poverty. Aspiration, according to Zipin, Sellar, Brennan and Gale, is a formative process that "entails capacities of human agency to desire, imagine, articulate and pursue alternative futures" (2015:230). These aspirations require the ability to read "a map of a journey into the future" (Appadurai 2004:76). While aspirations are relatively evenly held across different socio-economic groups, the *capacity to aspire*, which is shaped by social, cultural and economic experiences, requires the availability of what Appadurai (2004) calls 'navigational information' rather than individual motivation. The six students were able to articulate their desire to pursue futures that involved tertiary studies and a successful career but had little to no 'mapping' or 'navigational' information from their families that enabled them to envisage how these alternative futures could be achieved. Encouragement by their families to stay at school, work hard and pass each grade well was the only 'mapping' of their future goals that the students could offer.

In young people in low socio-economic contexts, aspirations are often grounded in what Zipin *et al* (2015), drawing on Bourdieu, describe as either a 'habituated' or 'doxic' logic. Habituated aspirations, drawing on Bourdieu's concept of 'habitus' (1984), reflect students' different structural positions in society that are derived from their biographical and historical conditions (i.e. their familial and socio-cultural groups), that tend to be reproduced. An example of this, is Willis's (1977) seminal study that followed twelve white, non-academic, UK working-class 'lads' in their school setting in the 1970s. These 'lads' rejected school and the value of education to focus on pursuing hands-on manual labour that, for them, was the cultural system of their working-class life. 'Doxic' aspirations, derived from Bourdieu's definition of 'doxa', refer to the out-workings of dominant beliefs and assumptions that circulate as natural and common sense. There are the norms to which we conform because there does not seem to be an alternative and which consequently frame our social lives (Webb, Schirato & Danaher 2002). 'Doxic' aspirations are therefore the aspirations with which students often respond when asked what they want to be when they grow up.

They are the responses that students know they should give based on what society values, what Bourdieu refers to as that which carries the most 'distinction' in society (Bourdieu 1984).

Zipin *et al* (2015:227) proffer a third alternative aspirational 'logic', one that provides for "emergent senses of future potential, grounded in lived cultures, which hold the possibility for imagining and pursuing alternative futures." What Zipin *et al* suggest within the field of education, is that these emergent future-orientated aspirations of students can be strengthened by drawing on the students' lifeworld identities, practices, knowledge and literacies. They refer to these as their Funds of Knowledge (FoK) (Moll, Amanti, Neff & Gonzalez 1992) from their homes and communities. Zipin *et al* draw on the FoK approach to suggest that those living in poverty have accumulated culturally developed bodies of knowledge, skills and literacies from their homes and community settings. They further suggest that these bodies of knowledge and skills, the students' lifeworld knowledge, if recognised and connected into the school learning process, hold the possibility to mediate different forms of learning practices that support the potential for emergent future-orientated aspirations for students living in impoverished circumstances.

The students' aspirations within their township school

The aspirations of the six students in the focus group were based on 'doxic' logic, i.e. what society values and deems distinctive, while at the same time showing aspects of the less tangible third logic of 'emergent' aspirations. They wanted to become doctors, scientists and engineers. These aspirations were linked to career paths that they perceived could offer them a better way of life, a pathway out of poverty, or as they stated: "To have a brighter future" (student discussion). When asked what it means to have a brighter or better future, one student stated: "It means to have and do good things, to help people like your family, and to love people and take care of them, like my parents. Like if anyone gets sick then I can help them … it also means convincing other children to study hard and not to quit school." Within these aspirations voiced by the students lies the emergent sense of future potential identified by Zipin *et al*, who state that emergent aspirations "are not primarily grounded in the past-made-present, but are emerging among young people as their lives apprehend the present-becoming-future" (2015:236).

However, with regard to understanding how to navigate the pathway that turns emergent aspirations into future possibilities, i.e. dreams and hopes into reality, Appadurai notes the following:

For the poor aspirational pathways are based on a smaller number of aspirational nodes and a thinner, weaker sense of the pathways from concrete wants to intermediate contexts to general norms and back again. Where these pathways do exist for the poor, they are likely to be more rigid, less supple, and less strategically valuable, not because of any cognitive deficit on the part of the poor, but because the capacity to aspire, like any complex cultural capacity, thrives and survives on practice, repetition, exploration, conjecture and refutation.   (2004:69)

Appadurai (2004) goes on to say that those living in poverty have what he calls "brittle horizons of aspirations" (p. 69) and therefore cultural recognition matters as "it is in culture that ideas of the future, as much of those about the past, are embedded and nurtured" (p. 59). Thus, in order to strengthen the 'capacity to aspire', i.e. a future- or emergent-orientated logic of possibilities of students within a marginalised school environment such as a township school, it is necessary to draw the cultural knowledge that has been embedded and nurtured within the students' home socialisations, into school knowledge. This might enable the "politics of recognition" (Taylor 1992) to find purchase among the issues of redistribution – or as Fraser suggests, in order that forms of redistribution are enhanced by issues of cultural recognition (Fraser 2001).

Discussing how students navigate their aspirations within the politics of recognition for social justice, Appadurai states:

The capacity to aspire ... through which poor people can effectively change the 'terms of recognition' within which they are generally trapped [involves disrupting] those rituals through which consensus is produced both among poor communities and between them and the more powerful. This process of consensus production is a crucial place to identify efforts to change the terms of recognition.   (2004:83)

Connecting the students' lifeworld knowledge to their school learning

What, therefore, does it mean for schools operating in a township context, to disrupt, interrupt and shift the terms of recognition on which education takes place? It can be argued that the 'process of consensus' is found within a particular educational discourse by which the South African school system is currently framed. This system that offers the belief that hard work and an imbibing of the knowledge encoded within the current narrow school curriculum will offer students upward mobility to achieve their aspirational goals. Interrupting or disrupting this 'process of consensus' requires teachers to find ways in which they can make school learning more culturally meaningful for students by acknowledging and including the students' lifeworld knowledges and social-cultural constructions of identity into the school learning process.

Within the student focus-group discussions, it was apparent that none of the six students realised that their cultural knowledge and literacies or out-of-school interests were forms of valuable knowledge. Thomson (2002) describes the knowledge, capacities and dispositions that students from less powerful groups bring to classrooms as their 'virtual school bags' (VSB). Hall and Thomson (2007:2–3) go on to say that "school only draws on the contents of some children's school bags", those that match the requirements of the school curriculum, while disregarding others. In other words, teaching those students that they are better off keeping their VSBs closed as the knowledge, skills and dispositions that they bring are not required or valued in the 'game of schooling' (Zipin 2013). For the six students, this was evident in their reluctance to discuss any knowledge or interests that were not related to school learning. One of the students stated that once, when he went on the computer at school, he got into trouble as he Googled cars because he wanted to find out about the first car that was made and also what future cars might look like. "They told me that we are not learning about cars at school, and I must practice my maths or get off the computer" (Sinethemba). This is an example of how school learning sends the message to students that their knowledge and interests are of little value in the school environment. Within the focus-group discussions, the students were almost confused by the invitation to 'unzip their VSB' and share its contents in the group (Zipin 2013).

The students' learning dispositions were founded on a form of passive receptivity to a particular form of school knowledge encoded in the curriculum. They were not used to being invited to share their thoughts, desires and dreams within the school learning context. In order to break the students' almost ritualised way of thinking, i.e. their disposition that school learning involves only the knowledge in the curriculum as found in their text books, the PLC dialogue centred around finding ways to use computers and the internet to change the 'terms of recognition' on which the schooling process is based. The PLC teachers were particularly concerned about finding ways to use technology to improve their students' use of English. The teachers taught a range of subjects such as English, Mathematics, Social Sciences, Natural Sciences and Technology. They felt that the biggest challenge in teaching in a township school was the change in the language of learning and teaching (LOLT) from isiXhosa in Grades 1–3 to English from Grade 4 onwards. Within the South African schooling context, as stated in the Bill of Rights, all students have the right to receive education in the official language of their choice. This right, however, is fettered by the state's ability to provide all students an education in their home language, given that South Africa has 11 official languages. Most schools choose either English or Afrikaans as the LOLT from Grade 4 upwards. What this means for teaching and learning in township schools, is that English is introduced to the students as their second language in Grades 1–3 and from Grade 4 onwards the LOLT changes to English in all subject areas. Students struggle with the transition of studying in Grades 1–3 in their home language, which in the Western Cape is usually isiXhosa, to studying only in English from Grade 4 onwards. This is exacerbated by the fact that in an impoverished township area such as Duduza, many students have a fairly limited exposure to English in their home and community environments.

In response to this challenge, the teachers in the PLC discussed finding ways to enrich the students' engagement with English by drawing on their students' knowledge and interests through the use of technology. The PLC teachers decided to begin the process by inviting a small group of Grade 6 students, which became the student focus group for the research project, to begin using the computers to complete a project about a topic of interest to the students. Each student was invited to choose their own project focus area, research information about their topic on the internet and type up their project on the computer. Initially the PLC teachers discussed using technology with all their students. However, the teachers felt a little overwhelmed regarding where to begin integrating technology into their lesson units due to their large classes and so the decision was taken to work with a small group of students first. In this way, the teachers felt that they would be better able to identify the challenges of using technology combined with a more open-ended approach that connected students' lifeworld knowledge and interests into school curriculum units, before opening the process up to an entire class. As facilitator of the PLC dialogue process and student focus group, I became involved in the process of the student discussion regarding their research project, as well as at times facilitating the students' research process using technology.

At the start of the student research project, I met with a student focus group to establish a possible research topic for each student. Initially the students were unable to consider topics outside of what they were currently learning at school and stated that they wanted to learn more about the topics they were learning about in class. However, none of the students could remember what they were learning in any of their subject areas – which in itself reveals how narrowly confined, constricted and unrelated school learning and school knowledge tends to be. The upside of this was that the students had to risk sharing their personal interests with the group, and as they tentatively began to open up, some potentially generative ideas flowed.

Sinethemba was the first student to venture his interests, which were closely linked to his aspirations, stating that he really wanted to learn more about history and also about the future as he wanted to become a scientist one day. He said: "I want to know about the past, what happened, and I also want to learn about the future ... I want to know about things, like what was the first car, what was the first animal on earth, about space and who went there first and about people going there now." A second boy, Aphiwe, a quiet and serious student, wanted to learn more about different countries. He noted specifically: "I am interested in learning about the UK, about their president, their homes, their schools, everything." This led to a conversation about why the United Kingdom (UK) had a prime minister and not a president; how and why their weather patterns are very different to those of South Africa; and even a discussion on how their schools differ from schools in South Africa. Further conversations revealed that Aphiwe aspires to live in the UK one day, stating that "it is far away, I want to go far away from here". Aphiwe currently lives with his aunt, brother and cousin in the township. His aspirations show that he positions himself within an emergent-future possibility that is far removed from the limitations of his current physical living conditions.

Sandisile, the third boy in the group, tentatively suggested that he wanted to research about a rapper who, it had been rumoured, had died in a car accident. He was desperate to find out if it was true or not. He seemed surprised when I agreed that this would be interesting to research. When Sandisile went on the internet and Googled the rapper who had apparently died, he found some sites that supported the story and other sites that said the story was a hoax. This required him to carefully read for the relevant information, drawing the other boys, who were equally interested, into the debate. At the end of the session I asked the students to give me feedback about what they had learned. Sandisile stated that he had learned that the rapper had not died, and that the internet did not always tell the truth.

The three girls' interests initially lay in researching about possible career options which they were quick to explain to me would help them know what to learn in school. Their aspirations included becoming a surgeon, a doctor and a medical scientist. They wanted to find out what subjects they would need to study, which universities they could go to and how much they would earn one day. They, however, found researching these career options very challenging as they realised that they knew nothing about their career choices which made the initial research activity very difficult without substantial input from an adult. As the aim of the research activity was for the students to use their interests to actively and independently find ways to use information from the internet to construct new knowledge, I encouraged the students to find slightly easier topics for the beginning stages of the process. When asked if there was anything they were interested in that perhaps was not related to school learning, they admitted that they wanted to find out about celebrities, the favourite being Beyoncé. They were, however, unsure that researching celebrities could be seen as a form of school learning and whether they would be allowed to do this during class time. After being assured that their teachers and principal had said that they could research anything they were interested in, they excitedly Googled sites that provided them with information and images of various celebrities. Even the boys left their research sites to be drawn into the girls' conversations about the lives of the various celebrities they Googled.

Engaging the students in conversation about the celebrities revealed that they were all well-informed about aspects of the celebrities' lives. This easily led into a discussion about one's life story which in turn provided the impetus for the students to begin to write their own life story, a task that the teachers identified as part of the CAPS requirements in the English 'Writing and Presenting' skill area. As this task was initially quite daunting for them, the teachers and I broke it into sections which included first writing about themselves, then about their homes and families, about their schooling, their likes and dislikes, and so forth. In the last section of their life story we encouraged them to imagine and write about their futures in order to give voice to their 'emergent' sense of future possibilities where they imagined alternative futures for themselves based on their aspirations. With the internet available to them, they discovered that there were many more future opportunities available to them than they had initially realised. Many of these were more realistic career options in line with their interests. As one of the girls noted: "I don't really want to be doctor because I know you have to study for a long time, and have to be very very clever, but I found other things that I can study and work in hospitals and help people." What was starting to happen was that as the 'terms of recognition' on which learning was based shifted, the students were able to move from 'doxic' to 'emergent'-orientated aspirations, which in turn motivated and provided them a form of agency in their own learning.

Mediants, mediating, materiality

In order to understand the role that the computers came to play in the students' shifting and changing learning dispositions, Appadurai states that there is a "relationship between mediation and materiality" and "[m]ediation, as an operation or embodied practice, produces materiality as the effect of its operations. Materiality is the site of what mediation – as an embodied practice – reveals" (2015:224). Thus, within the learning environment, the computers operated as a materiality that mediated (gave agency to) the shifting learning dispositions of the students. Agency, drawing on Appadurai, can be considered not only an action or intervention, but as the "site in which body, intention, action, and resistance come together" (2015:223). Appadurai goes on to state that it is important to understand that "materiality does not pre-exist mediation" (2015:225), but rather that the relationship between the two enables the co-production or working together as two sides of the same thing. Thus, within the context of teaching and learning, the computers came to act as a mediant that enabled, or gave agency to, the teachers and students as they began to shift to more open-framed teaching and learning practices.

By referring to the computers as a mediant, I suggest that the use of computers became an agentic device that changed how the teachers mediated the learning environment and how students began to shift their engagement with their learning, i.e. their learning dispositions. The computers also provided a wider, more open-ended resource that enabled the teachers to connect the students' school learning to culturally relevant and interesting material. The teachers' previous knowledge transfer had always taken place in a manner that was tightly sequenced, paced and framed by the CAPS and the text books provided by the Department of Education. Three of the teachers themselves had gone to school in the same township area where they were now teaching. While they had a keen understanding of the students' cultural context, they struggled to find ways to move beyond the current educational discourse that tends to frame teacher pedagogy in a particularly scripted and narrow way. What the computers provided was a learning space that was unfamiliar to both the teachers and the students, an almost empty stage on which new and different 'rituals' or 'processes of consensus' within the learning process could be formed.

It is at this point that the narrative concludes as the process currently rests in a new stage of experimentation, one that involves the teachers invoking the use of the computers as well as other potential materialities within the educational context to mediate a pedagogical relationship between alternative teaching practices and student learning dispositions. The shifts and changes that have taken place over a twelve-month period have been slow and small yet, I believe, significant. Just taking the students out of the classroom and into the computer room – changing the 'terms of recognition' on which teaching and learning were previously based – was a significant hurdle for the teachers to initially overcome.

In conclusion, I would like to be clear that I am not suggesting that using computers is the way to change teachers' pedagogical practices and student learning practices – although they might hold potential. The focus of this chapter is not on the use of technology, but on the role that it played as a mediant in shifting or changing the 'terms of recognition' on which learning takes place. What I suggest is that mediants, which could take any form, such as the FoK framework or material objects or resources, added meaningfully into the learning environment, hold the potential to mediate the social and the material so that new and different 'terms of recognition' can be established between teachers, students and the curriculum. Further, I propose, that it is by shifting or changing the 'terms of recognition' on which learning takes place, that it is possible to shift the 'doxic' aspirations of students living in poverty, into 'emergent' aspirations that are grounded in lived-cultural resources. This will enable students to enact their agency – to desire, imagine and pursue futures that hold the possibility of being turned into realities – within their learning practices in the school environment.

In the context of shifting and changing student learning dispositions, the chapter highlights the manner in which agency can be afforded to both materiality and individuals within aspects of teaching and learning. Appadurai states that it is necessary to "come to terms with the richness of the ways materiality can be reframed so as to expand our sense of … sociocultural processes more generally" (2015:224). In describing the manner in which the students engaged with their learning by developing a relationship between mediation (of their learning) and the materiality (computers) to construct new learning dispositions and learning practices, they support Appadurai's challenge to begin to develop "a richer and more robust theory of mediation, one that can accommodate our new-found interest in the range of vitalities, energies, and agencies within the ontologies of different human orders" (Appadurai 2015:224). In this way, it is then possible to begin to view students mediating their learning practices as a practice or assemblage of learning where materiality and mediation are seen to contain "mutual conditions of possibility and as effects of each other" (Appadurai 2015:233). What Appadurai wants us to consider, therefore, is that in order to address "problems of justice, power, and inequality in a world that is no longer composed exclusively of human agents", we must find ways within the educational context, to recognise that "materiality and mediation are always connected" (Appadurai 2015:235).

Fraser (2009) reminds that a social justice approach must involve an orientation that joins the redistribution of knowledge with an ethical consideration for the recognition of the students' diverse cultural knowledge and a representation of the diversity of the social-cultural groups in the process of knowledge selection. What this chapter has presented in response to Fraser's challenge, is the potential for teachers shifting the 'terms of recognition' on which the pedagogical process takes place by adapting their pedagogical practices to draw student identities, practices, knowledges and literacies from their homes and communities into the school knowledge code. This process, I suggest, holds the potential to shift student learning dispositions to include more hopeful investments in their school learning. In addition, it provides navigational material for 'emergent' aspirations that enable the students to enact agency by turning possibilities into realities in their educational becoming despite the constrained circumstances in which they currently reside.

References

Appadurai A. 2004. "The capacity to aspire: culture and the terms of recognition". In: V Rao & M Walton (eds). *Culture and public action*. California: Stanford University Press.

Appadurai A. 2015. Mediants, Materiality, Normativity. *Public Culture*, 27(2):221–237. https://doi.org/10.1215/08992363-2841832

Bourdieu P. 1984. *Distinction: A Social Critique of the Judgement of Taste*. Cambridge: Harvard University Press.

Bourdieu P. 1998. *Practical Reason: On the Theory of Action*. Stanford: Stanford University Press.

Fataar A. 2015. *Engaging schooling subjectivities across post-apartheid urban spaces*. Stellenbosch: AFRICAN SUN MeDIA. https://doi.org/10.18820/9781920689834

Fraser N. 2001. *Redistribution, recognition and participation: Toward an integrated conception of justice*. Paris: UNESCO Publications.

Fraser N. 2009. *Scales of Justice*. Cambridge: Polity Press.

Hall C & Thomson P. 2007. Creative partnerships? Cultural policy and inclusive arts practice in one primary school. *British Educational Research Journal*, 33(3):315–329. https://doi.org/10.1080/01411920701243586

Harrop-Allin S & Kros C. 2014. The C Major scale as index of 'back to basics' in South African education: A critique of the curriculum assessment policy statement. *Southern African Review of Education*, 20(1):70–89.

Hattam R, Brennan M, Zipin L & Comber B. 2009. Researching for social justice: contextual, conceptual and methodological challenges. *Discourse: Studies in the Cultural Politics of Education*, 30(3):303–316. https://doi.org/10.1080/01596300903037010

Hogg L. 2011. Funds of Knowledge: An investigation of coherence within the literature. *Teaching and Teacher Education*, 27(3):666–677. https://doi.org/10.1016/j.tate.2010.11.005

Maringe F, Masinire A & Nkambule T. 2015. Distinctive features of schools in multiple deprived communities in South Africa: Implications for policy and leadership. *Educational Management Administration & Leadership*, 43(3):363–385. https://doi.org/10.1177/1741143215570303

Moll L, Amanti C, Neff D & Gonzalez N. 1992. Funds of Knowledge for Teaching: Using a Qualitative Approach to Connect Homes and Classrooms. *Theory Into Practice*, 31(2):132–141. https://doi.org/10.1080/00405849209543534

Sayed Y & Motala S. 2012. Getting in and staying there: Exclusion and inclusion in South African schools. *South African Review of Education*, 18(2):105–118.

Statistics South Africa. *Census 2011*. http://www.statssa.gov.za [Accessed 16 September 2016].

Taylor C. 1992. *The ethics of authenticity*. United States of America: Harvard University Press.

Thomson P. 2002. *Schooling the rustbelt kids: making the difference in changing times*. Australia: Allen & Unwin.

Webb J, Schirato T & Danaher G. 2002. *Understanding Bourdieu*. Australia: Allen & Unwin.

Williams R. 1977. *Marxism and literature*. Oxford: Oxford University Press.

Willis P. 1977. *Learning to labour*. Farnborough: Saxon House.

Zipin L. 2013. Engaging middle years learners by making their communities curricular: A Funds of Knowledge approach. *Curriculum Perspectives*, 33(3):1–12.

Zipin L & Brennan M. 2006. Meeting Literacy Needs of Pre-service Cohorts: Ethical dilemmas for socially just teacher educators. *Asia-Pacific Journal of Teacher Education*, 34(3):333–351. https://doi.org/10.1080/13598660600927513

Zipin L, Fataar A & Brennan M. 2015. Can Social Realism do Social Justice? Debating the Warrants for Curriculum Knowledge Selection. *Education as Change*, 19(2): 9–36. https://doi.org/10.1080/16823206.2015.1085610

Zipin L, Sellar S, Brennan M & Gale T. 2015. Educating for Futures in Marginalized Regions: A sociological framework for rethinking and researching aspirations. *Educational Philosophy and Theory*, 47(3):227–246. https://doi.org/10.1080/001318 57.2013.839376

www.ingramcontent.com/pod-product-compliance
Lightning Source LLC
Chambersburg PA
CBHW080607090426
42735CB00017B/3358